Journey
out of the
Garden

St. *Francis*
of
Assisi
and the Process of
Individuation

Journey
out of the
Garden

St. Francis
of
Assisi

and the Process of
Individuation

Susan W.
McMichaels

PAULIST PRESS
New York / Mahwah, N.J.

The Publisher gratefully acknowledges the use of the following. Excerpts from *St. Francis of Assisi* (volumes I and II) by Thomas of Celano. Copyright 1963. Used by permission of Franciscan Herald Press. Excerpts from *C. G. Jung Lexicon: A Primer of Terms and Concepts* by Daryl Sharp. Copyright 1991. Used by permission of Inner City Books, Toronto. Excerpts from *Francis and Clare: The Complete Works,* edited and translated by Regis Armstrong, O.F.M. Cap. and Ignatius C. Brady, O.F.M. Copyright 1982. Used by permission of Paulist Press.

Scripture texts in this work are taken from the *New American Bible with Revised New Testament and Revised Psalms* © 1991, 1986, 1970 Confraternity of Christian Doctrine, Washington, D.C. and are used by permission of the copyright owner. All Rights Reserved. No part of the *New American Bible* may be reproduced in any form without permission in writing from the copyright owner.

Interior art courtesy of Alinari/Art Resource, New York

Cover design by Cindy Dunne

Library of Congress Cataloging-in-Publication Data

McMichaels, Susan, W.,   1946–
    Journey out of the garden : St. Francis of Assisi and the process of individuation / by Susan McMichaels.
        p.   cm.
    Includes bibliographical references.
    ISBN 0-8091-3726-7 (alk. paper)
    1. Francis, of Assisi, Saint, 1182–1226. 2. Christian saints—Italy—Assisi—Biography. 3. Individuation (Psychology)—Religious aspects—Christianity. I. Title.
BX4700.F6M3645   1997
271'.302—dc21
[B]   97-35893
                                                                                                  CIP

Published by Paulist Press
997 Macarthur Boulevard
Mahwah, New Jersey 07430

Printed and bound in the
United States of America

Contents

For John, Matthew, and Susan

ACKNOWLEDGMENTS

I am indebted to many wise and generous people for help with this book. I would like to thank Deborah Beckwith; Kristy Coats and my students at Claxton School; Allan Combs, Ileana Grams, and Robert Yeager at the University of North Carolina at Asheville; William Cook and the participants in the 1994 National Endowment for the Humanities seminar, "The Thirteenth Century 'Lives' of St. Francis of Assisi"; Allen Dec; Doug Fisher and Kathleen A. Walsh at the Paulist Press; Margaret Rose Simon Hall and Christy McCarley at the North Carolina Center for the Advancement of Teaching; Barbara and Walter Harriman; Ernest Leven; John, Matthew, and Susan McMichaels; Donald McNair; Nathaniel Reyburn; the St. Francis of the Hills Fraternity; Robert Salamone; Suzzy Sams; John, Michael, and Timothy Winship; and James and Llewellyn Woollcott.

CITATIONS

Thomas of Celano wrote two biographies of Francis as well as a treatise about his miracles. I have cited them as Celano I, Celano II, and Celano *Treatise,* followed by the number that refers to the section in which each quotation is located.

Daryl Sharp's *Lexicon* includes numerous quotations from the *Collected Works* of Carl Jung. I indicate this in my citations by putting the number of the volume of Jung's *Collected Works* in parentheses when Sharp is quoting Jung.

CHRONOLOGY

1181 or 1182. St. Francis of Assisi is born into the merchant class. He is baptized Giovanni di Pietro di Bernardone, but his father renames him Francesco.

1193 or 1194. St. Clare of Assisi is born into the noble class.

1198. Innocent III is elected pope. Duke Conrad of Urslingen's fortress, the Rocca, a symbol of imperial power, is razed by the people of Assisi. Innocent III gains control of the Duchy of Spoleto, which includes Assisi.

1199-1200. Civil war in Assisi leads to the destruction of castles and the end of feudalism. Clare's family is exiled to neighboring Perugia.

1202. War breaks out between Assisi and Perugia. Francis is taken prisoner during the Battle of Collestrada. He remains in prison for about a year until his father ransoms him.

1204. Francis suffers from a long illness. When he recovers (1204 or 1205), he sets out for Apulia to join the Crusade. In Spoleto he has a dream that compels him to return to Assisi.

1205. Clare returns to Assisi. Francis embraces a leper. He is told by a crucifix at the dilapidated church of San Damiano to rebuild the church. Taking this message quite literally, Francis takes some of his father's cloth and sells it, as well as his horse, in Foligno. He attempts to give the money to the priest at San Damiano, but the priest refuses to accept it. Francis leaves the money on a window ledge. His father is furious about the stolen cloth.

1206. Bishop Guido tries Francis in front of Santa Maria Maggiore. Francis returns the money from the stolen cloth, as well as all his clothes, to his father. He renounces his father, saying that his father is now in heaven. Bishop Guido covers Francis with his cloak. Francis finds some rough clothes and leaves Assisi for Gubbio, where he nurses lepers. In the summer he returns to Assisi and begins to repair San Damiano and two other churches around Assisi.

1207-1208. Francis continues to repair the churches. In the winter of 1208 he hears the gospel (Matthew 10) at Portiuncola, a tiny church below Assisi that he has been repairing, and discovers his vocation of evangelical poverty. Changing from a hermit's habit to the habit and rope cincture still worn by Franciscans, he begins to preach and is joined by seven other men. They go on three preaching missions.

1209. Francis and his friars return to Portiuncola. Joined by four more brothers, Francis writes a brief rule for his new order and goes to Rome seeking approval from Innocent III. Innocent gives them permission to preach poverty and be tonsured. The brothers spend some time at Orte and then settle in at Rivo Torto near Assisi.

1209 or 1210. A peasant chases the brothers out of Rivo Torto, so they return to Portiuncola. Francis changes the name of his group from *Penitents from Assisi* to *Lesser Brothers*. The Third Order of secular followers may have begun at this time.

1211. Francis attempts to join the crusade in Damietta, Syria, hoping for martyrdom, but is turned back by the weather.

1212. Clare runs away from her family and is accepted into the Franciscan Order at Portiuncola on Palm Sunday night. She is eventually installed at San Damiano, where she spends the rest of her life.

1213. Count Orlando of Chiusi gives Mount LaVerna to Francis as a hermitage.

1213-1214 or 1214-1215. Francis goes to Spain. Many nobles and scholars, including Thomas of Celano, enter the order.

1215. Francis goes to Rome for the Fourth Lateran Council.

1215 or 1216. Clare becomes the abbess of the Second Order of Franciscans, women who live a contemplative life of sisterhood in absolute poverty, institutional as well as individual.

1216. Innocent III dies. Honorius III is elected pope.

1217. Over five thousand friars meet for a General Chapter at Pentecost then disperse on missions beyond the Alps and overseas. Francis stays in Italy.

1219. Francis goes to Damietta and meets the sultan.

1220. Franciscan friars are martyred in Morocco. Francis goes to Acre and the Holy Land. He returns to Italy when he hears that there is dissension within the order. He resigns as head of the order (this may have happened a couple of years earlier), realizing that he has no administrative talent. He has Cardinal Hugolino (later Gregory IX) appointed protector of the order.

1221. Honorius III approves an official rule for the order. He may also have approved the rule for the Third Order at this time. Francis preaches in southern Italy and at Bologna.

1223. Francis composes the Second Rule at Fonte Colombo. He is under pressure from the church and the friars to relax the strictness of the First Rule, especially concerning radical poverty. The direction of the order is slipping from his grasp. Honorius approves the new rule. At Christmas, Francis organizes a midnight mass celebration that includes animals and a creche.

1224. A mission goes to England. Brother Elias has a vision that Francis will only live two more years. Francis goes to LaVerna for a forty-day fast during which he has a seraphic vision and receives the stigmata. He returns to Portiuncola. Then, though sick and weak, he makes a preaching tour through Umbria and the Marches that continues into 1225. Clare becomes ill although she will continue to live, in poor health, for twenty-nine more years.

1225. Francis visits Clare at San Damiano. His eyesight fails and he is bedridden. He composes the *Canticle of Brother Sun*. Cardinal Hugolino summons him to Rieti. He then goes to Fonte Colombo where his eyes are cauterized, but his condition does not improve.

1226. Francis's health is precarious. He spends time at Siena receiving unsuccessful treatment for his eyes. He returns to Assisi, where he is installed in the bishop's palace; but he insists on returning to Portiuncola when he realizes he is going to die. He sends a last letter to Clare and is visited by Lady Jacoba. He dies on October 3 at the Portiuncola. His body is brought to San Damiano before he is buried at San Giorgio in Assisi.

1227. Cardinal Hugolino becomes Pope Gregory IX.

1228. Gregory IX canonizes Francis and solicits funding for a basilica (which may have been designed by Brother Elias) in his honor. Thomas of Celano writes the first biography of Francis's life.

1230. Francis is transported to the basilica, an ironically grand memorial for a man who valued poverty and humility.

1232. Brother Elias is elected minister general of the Franciscan Order. (He will be deposed in 1239 because of his ostentatious lifestyle.)

1235. The first extant dossal (wood painted with a picture of a saint surrounded by episodes from his life) presents the new saint displaying his stigmata.

1243. Bonaventure enters the Franciscan Order.

1244. The friars are asked to gather more information about Francis, and their stories form the basis of Celano's second biography.

1253. Clare dies, leaving 150 monasteries of Poor Clares.

1257. John of Parma is asked to resign as minister general of the order because of his sympathy with the Spirituals, a group of friars who insist on radical poverty for the order and the church. Bonaventure, a moderate, becomes minister general.

1260-1263. Bonaventure writes an official biography of

Francis, and all previous accounts of the saint's life are suppressed.

1290-1295. Giotto (or his school) decorates the upper church of the basilica, using quotations from Bonaventure as the basis for the presentation of Francis to visiting pilgrims.

Introduction

Many people know Saint Francis of Assisi as a garden statue with a bird perched on his shoulder. Surrounded by the colors and scents of flowers and grass, he gently inspires a pleasant desire to live in harmony with nature and with each other. That Francis is part of the world we retreat to, rather than the world in which we live and work. Relegated to the garden and distanced from us by centuries of time, Francis's peaceful image presents no solution for our own frantic lives. Instead, he is a static cultural icon of unattainable gentleness and peace.

This book presents a different Francis. The Francis in this book struggled throughout his life to answer two simple questions: *Who are you, God, and who am I?* Francis's struggle yielded the mystic's answer: *We are one.* From the experience of this essential unity, Francis was transformed into the man of peace represented by the statue in the garden. But the statue in the garden shows only the destination; it does not show the path to the mystic's answer. This book attempts to follow Francis on his spiritual journey in the hopes of using him as our guide.

In our culture, Francis has been sentimentalized. If we are to use him as a potent symbol and guide, we must appreciate the struggle he underwent and be willing to undergo that same transformation. We must understand his journey as an example of the courage, balance, and compassion, as well as of the failures and shortcomings that we all experience as we try to move from the garden into the world and then back to the garden again. Francis's journey carried him through the turbulence of the thirteenth century into the darkness and illumination of his own soul. Our outer journey is taking place in a different, but equally turbulent historical context; the inner journey is timeless. Francis can guide us on both journeys; for in spite of his distance from us in time and culture, his thirteenth-century spiritual journey can be made accessible to us if we place it within a modern, psychological framework.

The psychological dimension of the mystic's journey is called *individuation,* a process that was first described by Carl Jung. In the course of his clinical work, as well as in his investigation of world cultures and mythologies, Jung gathered empirical evidence that a force compels individuals to break away from the assumptions learned from family and society and to develop a unique way of looking at and living out their lives. These individuals cannot be satisfied with other people's answers to the question of life's meaning. They must look deeper by asking, What is the meaning of *my* life? If the individual is both brave enough to break from the group consensus and strong enough to accept who s/he really is, an authentic personality is created. This unique personality can then help others discover their own uniqueness.

To Jung, Christ was one of the best examples of individuation in human history: "This apparently unique life became a sacred symbol because it is the psychological prototype of the only meaningful life, that is of a life that strives for the individual realization—absolute and unconditional—of its own particular law."[1] Francis's importance for us is that he strove to emulate Christ by discovering and expressing his own unique role in creation. We need to remember and be impressed by Francis because of his absolute and unconditional willingness to be himself, which means his unconditional willingness to express God's will by living as honestly and consciously as possible.

The validity of using Jung's twentieth-century insights to interpret a thirteenth-century life is based on the assumption, shared by both mysticism and depth psychology, that there is a commonality in human experience that transcends space and time. Carl Jung discovered that a dimension of the human psyche, which he called the *collective unconscious,* produces religious symbols. In the thirteenth century, these symbols resonated with meaning within the framework of Christianity. In Jung's time and our own, religion no longer provides a framework of meaning for many people in our culture. Unable to find significance in religious symbols within the framework of organized religion, people are forced to develop their own religious myths to lend meaning to their lives, or else they may experience depression and despair. However, both in medieval Christianity and in Jung's twentieth-century psychological theory, powerful symbols insist on recognition through individual lives. Like the Christian belief system, Jung's psychological theory of individuation offers Christ as the exemplar of the process of human salvation, both in individual and collective terms. The life of Francis is important to us as an example of one man who, by suffering the process of individuation, made Christ a living symbol in his own life and in the lives of others.

While acknowledging the importance of different cultural contexts, this book implicitly refutes the claim of historical contextualists who contend that "practices and symbols of any culture are so imbedded in that culture as to be inseparable from it."[2] Instead, it proceeds on the assumption that "archetypal experience refuses the constraints of time and space and, to some extent, culture. This would mean that [Saint Francis's] experiences in the thirteenth century and Jung's in the twentieth proceed from those layers of the collective psyche which transcend the confines of time and space."[3] Thus this book demonstrates the essential identity of meaning between the Jungian process of individuation and Francis of Assisi's spiritual journey and presents both as complementary visions of the fully realized life. We will begin with a brief account of Francis's life to orient the reader for the discussion that follows.

In 1181 or 1182, Giovanni di Pietro di Bernardone was baptized in Assisi, a small Italian hill town in the province of Umbria. Francis's mother named him Giovanni for John the Baptist. She believed from the start that her son would have a special, prophetic affinity for Christ. However, when his father Pietro returned from a business trip, he renamed his son Francesco. Francis's father was a cloth merchant who often traded in southern France. Perhaps his fondness for France explains Pietro's giving his son the unusual name of Francesco. Coming from Provence herself, Francis's mother shared her husband's love for southern France. She gave her son a passion for the French songs of the troubadours, songs that Francis later adapted to joyfully praise God and creation.

Francis grew up in rooms attached to his father's shop near the main square of Assisi. He went to school at nearby San Giorgio but was never much of a scholar. His Latin was always poor; he had more success writing in the Umbrian vernacular as he did when he composed the *Canticle of Brother Sun* near the end of his life.

When Francis was eleven or twelve, a girl was born into Assisi's nobility in a handsome building on the square of San Giorgio. Her name was Clara Offreduccio. We know her as Saint Clare. She was to play a crucial role in Francis's spiritual journey.

Although Francis and Clare probably knew each other by sight as children, they were separated by the class warfare that erupted in Assisi at the end of the twelfth century. As the development of capitalism put money into the hands of the emerging middle class, civil war broke out against the nobles. The Rocca, a fortress above the city, and the surrounding castles were razed. Assisi's nobility, including Clare's family, were forced to flee to nearby Perugia.

After the merchants and artisans gained political control in Assisi, war broke out between Assisi and Perugia. Francis was taken prisoner during a battle between the two cities and spent a year in a Perugian prison. His health broken by imprisonment, he returned to Assisi weak, depressed, and introspective. The young man who had previously led his friends through the streets of Assisi, carousing and singing bawdy songs, spent a year languishing in his father's house. He was nursed by his mother, who sensed in him the beginnings of a transformation. His father, however, was anxious for the return of the former Francis, who had helped out in the shop and advertised the family's financial success by wearing luxurious clothes and lavishly entertaining his friends.

Francis recovered from his long illness in 1204 or 1205, during the same time that Assisi's noble families began returning from Perugia. His father outfitted him as a knight so he could join the forces preparing to set out on a Crusade from Apulia on the coast of Italy. Francis wanted to return to his old, carefree life as the popular son of a rich merchant, but he began having dreams and visions that compelled him to attend to his inner journey. Francis was embarking on the process of individuation.

Clare, along with the rest of Assisi, watched with interest when the flamboyant Francis turned back from the expedition to Apulia and found himself unable to resume his former life. In the noisy, public life of Assisi, everyone was aware of the tension growing between Francis and his father. They knew things were going badly when Francis's father locked him in the cellar and his mother helped him escape. So when the news went around that Francis's father had charged him with stealing some cloth that the towns-people knew Francis had sold to buy materials to rebuild a dilapidated church outside of Assisi, everyone assembled in the courtyard in front of the cathedral for Francis's trial. Before the bishop and the townspeople of Assisi, including twelve-year-old Clare, Francis repudiated his father, return-ing his money and even all his clothes.

In this dramatic and literal way, Francis stripped himself of his former life and persona. He continued repairing churches around Assisi for the next two years. Then, in the winter of 1208, he discovered his vocation of evangelical poverty while listening to Matthew 10, in which Jesus com-missions the twelve apostles to go forth preaching peace and the presence of God's kingdom. Jesus admonishes the apostles: "Do not take gold or silver or copper for your belts; no sack for the journey, or a second tunic, or sandals, or walking stick" (Mt.10:9).[4] Francis believed that the gospel was addressing him directly, and he immediately designed a uniform to express his newly found vocation of evangelical poverty—the habit and rope cincture still worn by Franciscans. Soon his followers numbered twelve.

The next years saw the birth of the Franciscan Order. As Francis suffered the process of individuation, his unique personality became a powerful instrument for change. Men and women of all classes were attracted to his life of radical poverty. In 1212, Clare ran away from her family and was accepted into the Franciscan Order. She became the leader of an order of contemplative women living in absolute poverty. By 1217 Franciscan friars, with their evangelical mission, numbered more than five thousand and traveled far beyond Europe. The Franciscan movement had a secular order as well, with its own rule for a life of evangelical poverty while living and working in the world.

Francis had no vocation or talent as an administrator. By 1220 he resigned as head of the order. He continued to alternate between periods of solitude and contemplation and intense preaching missions. During periods of contemplation, he experienced the drama of Christ's life and death happening within his own psyche. He honored that revelation by developing a new kind of mysticism, rooted in imaginative interaction between the seeker and events in the life of Christ. Francis shared his new kind of mysticism in the tiny village of Grecchio in 1223. There he enacted a living crèche during midnight mass. The following year, on the remote mountain of LaVerna, Francis's compassionate, imaginative experience of Christ's crucifixion resulted in his receiving the stigmata.

Blind and in extremely poor health, Francis lived for two more years. In 1225, while staying at Clare's cloister, he wrote the *Canticle of Brother Sun* as an expression of the mystic unity he experienced during his spiritual journey. He died on October 3, 1226, at the Portiuncola, the little church outside Assisi where he first came to realize his vocation of evangelical poverty twenty-two years before, and was buried in San Giorgio. Two years later he was canonized, and two years after that his body was transported to a basilica built to commemorate his extraordinary spiritual journey.

Each chapter in this book examines an aspect of Francis's psycho-spiritual journey in the context of psychological individuation. A glossary of terms (pp. 152–158) provides definitions for the psychological language that may be unfamiliar to the reader. Chapter 1 looks at the church as the most important institutional source of collective values in the thirteenth century and shows how these values both helped and hindered Francis's spiritual development. Chapter 2 considers *adaptation* as the prologue to individuation. It shows how Francis came to accept his father's plans for his life and to fit into life in Assisi before he realized that his life must go in a very different direction. Chapter 3 examines Francis's conversion in terms of *persona*. Francis's persona suited the well-adjusted person he appeared to be until his early adulthood. After his conversion experience, he learned, slowly and painfully, that he was not really the person his father and the townspeople of Assisi knew and loved. He adopted a new persona that better expressed his inner life and beliefs. Chapter 4 introduces the *shadow*, both in terms of the personal and the collective unconscious. The shadow is the part of our personality and of our culture that we do not feel comfortable looking at and accepting. We tend to overlook what we find unacceptable in ourselves and notice it in other people instead. Francis had to struggle to accept every part of himself and of those around him. Like the rest of us, he was only partially successful, but both his successes and his failures can help us better understand the problem of the shadow in our own lives. The focus of chapter 5 is an exploration of Francis's *anima*, the feminine aspect of his psycho-spiritual nature. Like all men, Francis first became acquainted with his anima through the important women in his inner and outer life—his mother, Clare, Lady Jacoba, the Virgin Mary, and Lady Poverty.[5] In chapter 6 we explore Francis's psycho-spiritual journey using Jung's model of psychological orientation. Chapter 7 examines Francis's seraphic vision and stigmatization, both as historical phenomena and as evidence of the flow of energy between Francis's conscious and unconscious psyche. Chapter 8 considers the *Canticle of Brother Sun* as a document of the growth of consciousness that occurred during Francis's psycho-spiritual journey. The final chapter considers Francis as a heroic example of individuation.

In our culture, we idolize the Francis who wrote the *Canticle of Brother Sun,* a hymn to the goodness and unity of creation and the Creator. We skip over the Francis in chapter 7, who struggled in solitude and was wounded by his identification with Christ. As we move through the book, we will try, with Francis, to earn the serenity of the statue in the garden by suffering, with him, the process of individuation.

Our understanding of Francis's spiritual journey is based on his own writing, as well as on medieval hagiography (lives of saints), legends, art, and modern historical scholarship. Medieval writers and artists presented Francis as a new kind of saint, one whose stigmata attested to a deeper level of intimacy between God and humans. Whether or not all the details of his life and miracles withstand our standards for biographical accuracy, the impact of Francis's unique personality on the thirteenth century and beyond is irrefutable. The legend of his life that we glean from surviving records is the story of a man who found God's will for his life by first turning inward and then living his inner vision in the outer world.

CHAPTER ONE
Collective Values in the Thirteenth Century

Francis evolved into a unique human being within the context of medieval Christianity. This was a mixed blessing. On the positive side, the sacramental life of the church and the language and imagery of the Bible provided a rich system of symbols and rituals to actualize Francis's spiritual journey. On the negative side, he had to stay within parameters acceptable to the church or be labeled a heretic. A little historical background will help us understand Francis's journey in the context of the medieval church.

The church was the most powerful collective spiritual and secular force in the medieval world. The Gregorian reform in the middle of the eleventh century facilitated the centralization of political and ecclesiastical authority in Rome and widened the gap between the clergy and the laity. The bureaucratic, hierarchical organization of the church undermined the autonomy of the clergy and bishops and gave the papacy more power to confront the emperor of the Holy Roman Empire and other secular authorities. At the same time, the clergy's distance from and power over the laity was increased by clerical celibacy, the exclusive right to preach, and the power to consecrate the eucharist, a sacrament that grew in importance when the doctrine of transubstantiation was defined by Innocent III at the Fourth Lateran Council in 1215.[6]

Innocent III, who came to power in 1198 when Francis was sixteen, took full advantage of the papacy to become the most powerful man in the Western world. His interference in Assisi is an example of the scope of political activities undertaken by the church. In 1199, in an attempt to wrest control of Assisi from Emperor Otto, Innocent recalled the imperial representative from the Rocca, the chief fortification overlooking the city. The people of the city, young Francis probably among them, took advantage of the power vacuum in Assisi to storm the Rocca and raze it, installing a government independent of emperor or pope. After this uprising thwarted his plans to control Assisi, Innocent favored Perugia, Assisi's archenemy just across the valley, which further exacerbated the long-standing hostility between the two cities. Then in 1212, Innocent was instrumental in deposing Emperor Otto and installing Frederick II, who had been his ward. The struggle for power between the Guelphs, supported by the papacy, and the opposing Ghibelline faction violently polarized Italian cities throughout (and beyond) Francis's lifetime.[7]

Another way Innocent III contributed to both the power of the papacy and the polarization of the medieval world was through the Crusades, launched at the end of the eleventh century to win the Holy Land back from the Moslems. The Fourth Crusade, under Innocent III, was intended by Innocent to be waged against the Moslems in Jerusalem, but resulted instead in the pillaging of Constantinople and the establishment of a Latin empire in the East. The Christian world was polarized between East and West.[8]

Innocent III also initiated violence against the Cathars in southern France to eliminate the growth of heresy as a threat to the authority of the church. The Cathars believed that spirit was good and the human body and physical matter bad. They were not Christians because they did not accept the possibility of the incarnation of Christ. They believed that an evil God created the physical world, and the good God controlled the spiritual world. Their goal was to transcend the physical world by practicing extreme asceticism. Albigensianism, the Cathars' variation of dualism, was brutally suppressed at the same time that the Franciscan asceticism and poverty were being accepted by Innocent III. Innocent realized that Francis's combination of personal charisma and institutional loyalty could channel some of the popular piety that otherwise threatened the authority of the church. Francis thus became a weapon in the pope's war against heresy.

The Cathars were among several lay movements that sprang up in the twelfth and thirteenth centuries as people sought spiritual autonomy from the power and corruption of the church. The Beguines and Waldensians are examples of such movements. The Beguines were groups of women who lived lives of devotion and charity without being bound by any official vows of the church. Their movement originated in the twelfth century in Belgium and the Netherlands and spread through France and Germany. The Beguine communities were often broken up by the church in the thirteenth and fourteenth centuries out of fear that heresy would be fostered by popular expressions of piety. The Waldensians were a twelfth-century movement that was quickly labeled heretical. In 1174, eight years before Francis was born, Peter Waldo dedicated himself to a life of poverty and criticized the wealth of the church and the indifference of the clergy. His movement, which prefigured Franciscanism in its radical espousal of poverty, was condemned by the church ten years later. Francis had to create a way to express his vision of Christian living without

threatening the authority of the church. The tension
between his individual calling and the collective authority
of the church engendered a new kind of Christian life, that
of the mendicant friar.

Prior to Francis's creation of the role of mendicant friar,
preaching and living a life of poverty in the secular world,
monks were physically, and to a large extent spiritually
cloistered from the world.[9] Monasticism was the repository
of a mystical tradition and the source of periodic church
reform. The monastic tradition sanctioned a personal
encounter with the God within, as well as the God accessed
through the sacramental life of the church. Bernard of
Clairvaux, the twelfth-century Cistercian who reformed his
order and helped launch the Second Crusade, exemplifies
the mystical tradition in monasticism when he says, in a sermon on the *Song of Songs:* "Today the text we are going to
study is the book of our own experience. You must therefore take your attention inward, each one must take note of
his own particular awareness."[10]

Francis's psycho-spiritual journey moved Bernard's intimate, personal experience of God out of the monastic walls
and into the secular world. Francis combined the contemplative life of the monk with the active life of a lay preacher.
At the same time, he worked to reform the church by set-
ting an example of poverty, humility, and sacramental living. Francis became a peacemaker within a church that
waged and fomented war, a beggar whose poverty was
endorsed by a church reviled for its wealth, and, when he
received the stigmata, a source of grace within a church
that controlled and defined the flow of grace.

The thirteenth-century church taught that God was
essentially transcendent. Francis helped his age rediscover
God's immanence in the physical world and in each individual soul. That awareness was muted first by the church

and later by the secular *isms* of scientific rationalism, individualism, and materialism that still inform collective beliefs today. Like Francis at the end of the medieval era, we are rediscovering spirit in matter and in the unconscious. Our collective beliefs are being challenged by scientific discoveries in physics and psychology about the mutability of matter and the power of the unconscious. Francis's personal experience of God's <u>immanence</u> can help us understand the transformation in our perception of the world today. *existing in all parts of the universe*

Francis's capacity to modify collective values in the thirteenth century morally justified his process of individuation in the context of medieval Christianity and saved him from being labeled a heretic. Jung articulated this social responsibility that is implicit in the individuation journey: "Without this production of values, final individuation is immoral....Not only has society a right, it also has a duty to condemn the individuant if he fails to create equivalent values."[11] When the "creation of equivalent values" achieves positive collective recognition, the individuant becomes a cultural hero—in Francis's case, a saint.

Sainthood in the early church resulted from martyrdom for the faith. When being a Christian became less physically perilous, new paths to sainthood, through living rather than losing one's life, evolved. However, until the twelfth century, saints generally had to be monastic or clerical, or else members of the nobility. With the breakdown of feudalism and the emergence of popular piety in the twelfth and thirteenth centuries, nonaristocratic lay people were sometimes considered for sainthood.

Sainthood in the age of faith did not mean what it means in our thoroughly secularized world—a life of perfection. Rather, it was a life that expressed one of a variety of responses to Christ. In the introduction to *Images of Sainthood in Medieval*

Europe, Brigitte Cazelles describes medieval sainthood as "a plurality of responses to manifestations of Christian faith."[12] Medieval sainthood was a unique expression of individual personality sanctioned by the collective values of the church. Because Francis's process of individuation was intelligible within the paradigm of medieval sanctity, he was canonized as an exemplar of an authentic response to the life of Christ. Had his journey been perceived by the church as taking him too far from collective values, he would have been labeled a heretic. It was part of Francis's genius to be able to express, through his life, values that the church needed if it were to survive as a vehicle of spirituality. Whereas other reformers were labeled heretics and were destroyed by Innocent III and his successors, Francis introduced and institutionalized a new spirituality that helped reshape collective values in the thirteenth century and that can help us rediscover spiritual values in our postmodern age.

CHAPTER TWO
Adaptation as the Merchant's Son

Before Francis could begin his individuation journey, he needed the experience of standing on solid ground. Ideally, the values of our parents and society give us confidence, illusory though it may prove to be, that the ground beneath our feet is firm and real. Our individuation journey may radically transform our understanding of the terrain, but we cannot take the first step of the journey until we have confidence about where to step. Thus the confidence that precedes the uniqueness of individuation develops, paradoxically, through social conformity. Jung explains the necessity for conformity preceding individuation through the image of a plant: "If a plant is to unfold its specific nature, it must first grow in the soil in which it is planted."[13]

Francis accepted the authority and teaching of the medieval church. His spiritual journey took place within the parameters of medieval Christianity. He never consciously rejected any aspect of the church. We will see that later many of his followers interpreted his experience as signaling the need for a break with the traditional church; however, Francis never made such an assertion. He understood his spiritual journey as a calling to rebuild and repair the existing church, not to replace it with something new. Francis was able to discover and express his spirituality partly because the soil of medieval Christianity was well suited to

17

his individual growth requirements. We will consider, in the course of this book, whether his conscious adaptation to medieval Christianity stunted some of his authentic responses to people, situations, and his own spirituality. For the moment, however, we will examine his adaptation, as a child and as a young man, to his own family situation.

Francis was planted in the late twelfth century into a merchant family. His father espoused the materialistic values of the newly emerging middle class; his mother believed in the primacy of the spiritual life. The conflicting values in his family could have prevented Francis from taking root as an individual if he had consciously vacillated between his mother and his father. However, his father's more forceful personality, coupled with his traditional authority, caused Francis to put down his conscious roots in the violent, materialistic soil of his father's times rather than in the spiritual, otherworldly soil of his mother's. The spiritual dimension of his personality was repressed.

The necessary process of conforming to one set of values by repressing others is called, in psychological language, *adaptation.* The plant that develops through the process of adaptation is the *ego,* the "I" that provides a sense of continuity to the journey through life and enables one to have the strength to undergo the individuation process. Building on Jung's naturalistic imagery, we can better understand Francis's need for ego adaptation. Without deep roots in the soil, the onslaught of the elements during individuation—the stripping away of the petals of the *persona,* the overwhelming darkness of the *shadow,* freakish weather from *anima* attacks, the constant rain of tears, and the searing sun of *consciousness*—would rapidly destroy the ego-plant and with it the potential for a unique contribution.

During childhood and adolescence, Francis planted himself firmly as his father's son. However, this adaptation took its toll. Everything about Francis that was not defined by his father and his father's values had to be repressed. It all went underground into Francis's *personal unconscious.* So while the process of adaptation develops an ego strong enough to survive the process of individuation, it also—again paradoxically—creates many of the elements that lie buried in the unconscious, waiting to be painfully grafted onto consciousness. Adaptation contributes to the creation of the personal unconscious that Jung describes as the repository of "lost memories, painful ideas that are repressed,...subliminal perceptions,...and contents that are not yet ripe for consciousness."[14]

What were the values that Francis adapted to as his ego was being formed? Capitalism was breaking down the medieval social and political system of feudalism in Italy, a centuries-old system in which the three classes of clergy, nobility, and serfs were bound together by an elaborate web of interdependence and mutual obligation. Francis was born into the newly emerging middle class. The values of this class, and the political system it developed in opposition to feudalism, were rooted in capitalistic materialism. Francis and his father probably participated in the overthrow of the nobility in Assisi, when Francis was sixteen, and the establishment of a commune to rule the city independent of control from either the emperor or the pope. Arnaldo Fortini, the mayor of Assisi during World War II and a prodigious historian of Francis in the context of medieval Assisi, describes the soil of this new economic system as "rooted in a mania for material gain, a desire for commercial expansion."[15]

Francis adapted to his socially defined role as the spoiled, pampered son of a nouveau riche merchant. He dressed well, entertained lavishly, and despised lepers, society's outcasts who had no value in a capitalistic system of exchange.

Celano describes Francis as growing up in a culture where "people seek to educate their children from the cradle on very negligently and dissolutely."[16] He adds, "Indeed, he outdid all his contemporaries in vanities and he came to be a promoter of evil and was more abundantly zealous for all kinds of foolishness. He was the admiration of all and strove to outdo the rest in the pomp of vainglory, in jokes, in strange and useless talk, in songs, in soft and flowing garments."[17] Celano describes Francis's striving to avoid the unpleasant aspects of life in Assisi, particularly lepers: "So greatly loathesome was the sight of lepers to him...that...he would look at their houses only from a distance of two miles and he would hold his nostrils with his hands."[18]

In addition to dressing well, playing hard, and despising social outcasts, Francis shared his father's desire to rise into the nobility by becoming a knight. Knighthood was the path that the new middle class could follow to embellish their wealth with a patina of respectability. In 1204, outfitted in great style by his father, Francis set out on an expedition to Apulia to join Walter of Brienne's forces in the Fourth Crusade.

The year preceding the expedition was marked by the first indication that Francis's adaptation was beginning to break down. Francis suffered a long bout of depression. Depression often signals unconscious anger about the way adaptation to life is forcing us to deny our unique reality. However, once the symptoms of depression are somewhat relieved, we usually return to the status quo. Francis's experience in 1203 and 1204 followed this familiar pattern.

Francis was nursed through his long illness by his mother, who represented a different value system from that of his father. She had a spiritual nature in contrast to the materialism of Francis's father. In *The Second Life of St. Francis,* which presents a more idealized account of both the young Francis and his mother than the first biography, Celano compares Francis's mother to Elizabeth, the mother of John the Baptist. Celano says that she named Francis Giovanni (John) because she intuited the special relationship he would have with Christ. The biographical accuracy of this revision is not important. What is interesting is that Celano, in pondering on the meaning of Francis's life, needed to establish a tension between the mother and father to explain the tension between Francis's initial adaptation to his father's values and his later spiritual transformation. Francis had to emphasize the masculine side of his nature while he was becoming a man but needed the feminine side, first experienced through his mother, to embark on individuation. This need to integrate one's contrasexual nature will be more fully explored in a later chapter. It is a cornerstone of Jungian psychology, but it is also a spiritual insight from medieval times that was incorporated by Celano into the Francis legend.

Francis could not live by his mother's spiritual values while he was becoming a man. His father renamed him Francis instead of John, perhaps in recognition of the lucrative cloth trade in France; Francis developed a conscious attitude, in the course of adapting to his external environment, that accorded with his father's value system. However, his mother's spiritual values and intuitive nature would emerge in the course of individuation.

Besides her spirituality, Francis's mother, who may have been from Provençe, gave him a love of the music of the troubadours. Troubadours were aristocratic poets and musicians who emerged in Provençe as part of the cultural response to the relative peacefulness of the eleventh and twelfth centuries. Until the Albigensian Crusade destroyed the civilization of Provençe, the code of chivalry and courtly love was expressed in the songs of the troubadours.

Francis was able to include this aspect of his mother's culture into his social adaptation because it fit in with his adaptation as the merchant's son. Part of Francis's persona in Assisi was to be a singer of these songs as he roamed the streets of Assisi with his friends late at night or entertained them at parties. Besides singing with his friends, Francis led the *Tripudianti,* a group that performed traditional dances for religious and secular festivals as well as for tournaments and jousts. Francis's love of singing and dance would help express his authentic personality throughout the process of individuation.

The tension between the values of his mother and those of his father, handled by repression of his mother's spiritual values during adaptation, emerged during individuation as a struggle of opposites. In the novel *Saint Francis,* Kazantzakis dramatizes this struggle in an exchange between Francis and his closest companion, Brother Leo:

> About my mother and father, Brother Leo. The two of them have been wrestling inside me for ages. The struggle has lasted my whole life—I want you to realize that. They may take on different names—God and Satan, spirit and flesh, good and bad, light and darkness—but they always remain my father and mother. My father cries within me: "Earn money, get rich, use your gold to buy a coat of arms, become a nobleman. Only the rich and the nobility deserve to live in the world. Don't be good; once you're good, you're finished! If someone chips one tooth in your mouth, break his whole jaw in return. Do not try to make people love you; try to make them fear you. Do not forgive: strike!"...And my mother, her voice trembling within me, says to me softly, fearfully, lest my father hear her: "Be good, dear Francis, and you shall have my blessing. You must love the poor, the humble, the oppressed. If someone injures you, forgive him!" My mother and father wrestle within me, and all my life I have been struggling to reconcile them. But they refuse

to become reconciled; they refuse to become reconciled, Brother Leo, and because of that, I suffer.[19]

Francis first consciously suffered the opposites personified by his father and mother when his adaptation to life as the son of Pietro Bernardone began to come apart. The breakdown of his adaptation is the subject of the next chapter.

CHAPTER THREE
Stripping Off the Persona

Adaptation to family and society requires the development of a *persona,* a term that derives from the Greek word for 'mask.' Persona is the identity we develop—first in our family and later in school, on the job, and in our other social interactions. One's persona, which determines one's conscious standpoint and behavior, inevitably leaves out many dimensions of a person's wholeness. Much of what one truly *is* must be repressed in the interest of getting along in the world. As Jung expressed it, "[persona] is a compromise between individual and society as to what a man should appear to be."[20]

In Greek drama when an actor assumed the mask of the person s/he was portraying, the mask was fixed throughout the performance. No individual nuance of expression was possible. This etymology helps us understand the positive and negative effects of persona on our own lives. Like the actor's mask, our persona enables others to identify us easily and know what to expect from us. Our persona also enables us to react automatically to people and situations. But like the inflexible actor's mask, persona can also limit the scope of interpretation we give to our own lives and prevent others from seeing us in all our complexity. In the positive sense, persona enables us to maintain a sense of personal continuity so that we and those with whom we

interact know what to expect. It enables us to carry out our
various roles in life—as parent, spouse, friend, worker, or
whatever other roles we play—in a way that is consistent and
comprehensible. But a persona can become a mask for the
person we really are, a mask that we forget to remove when
we look into the mirror of our own unique soul. That is why
the process of individuation often forces us to strip off our
persona.

Francis had a considerable stake in his persona. It was his
way of relating to his father, his peers, and society at large,
as well as his conception of himself. It was his guarantee of
worldly success and his basis for self-confidence. So it took
the unconscious force that precipitates the process of individuation a good deal of energy and time to overcome Francis's attachment to the young man he had been. His illness
after prison was the beginning. During illness a general feeling of lassitude enervates the will, making it easier for the
unconscious to assert itself. Depression is common.[21] Francis emerged from his illness in a depressed state.

Francis's illness was preceded by several years of violence in Assisi. In 1198 the citizens of Assisi destroyed the
Rocca as a symbol of the imperial presence. For the next
two years, a civil war resulted in the destruction of feudal
castles and the establishment of the commune. In 1202,
when Francis was twenty, war broke out between Assisi and
neighboring Perugia, Assisi's traditional enemy. Francis
was taken prisoner during the particularly violent Battle of
Collestrada and was imprisoned for a year before being
ransomed by his father.

The two years that Francis was isolated from his normal
activities and relationships may have precipitated the
depression that followed his illness. The atrocities that he
witnessed during civil war in Assisi and in the war with
Perugia may also have begun to weaken his persona. His

first biographer saw God's hand in Francis's illness and depression: "Suddenly the divine vengeance, or, perhaps better, the divine unction, came upon him and sought first to recall his erring senses by visiting upon him mental distress and bodily suffering....Thus, worn down by a long illness...he began to think of things other than he was used to thinking upon."[22] Bonaventure, the minister general of the Franciscan Order who wrote an official biography of Francis that supplanted earlier accounts, also saw purpose in Francis's illness: "God afflicted his body with a prolonged illness in order to prepare his soul for the anointing of the Holy Spirit."[23]

Jung also sees intentionality in psychological events that precipitate a new way of thinking: "The psyche does not merely *react,* it gives its own specific answer to the influences at work upon it."[24] The unconscious is seeking recognition and integration by the conscious ego. What Celano calls "the divine unction," Jung calls the *Self,* the psychospiritual reality of "the God within us."[25]

"The God within" was calling Francis to begin the process of individuation by undercutting his previous adaptation and directing his psychic energy inward so that the exterior world temporarily lost its attraction. "The beauty of the fields, the pleasantness of the vineyards, and whatever else was beautiful to look upon, could stir in him no delight," wrote Celano.[26]

Although Francis no longer delighted in the physical beauty of Umbria, he still had an interest in maintaining his persona, which he expressed through the clothes he wore. Sumptuously outfitted in knightly regalia purchased by his father, he planned an expedition to Apulia to join Walter of Brienne's forces in the Fourth Crusade. But before Francis left Assisi, two significant persona events occurred. He gave away some of his clothes, and he had a vision of knightly armor. Giotto (or members of his school)[27] depicted both of these events among the twenty-eight frescoes painted at the end of the thirteenth century in the upper church of the basilica in Assisi. Giotto's version of Francis's generosity is based on Bonaventure's biography of Francis, *La Legenda Maior,* written in the 1260's. The inscription from Bonaventure below the fresco reads: "When Francis chanced to meet a nobleman destitute and poorly clothed he was moved by compassion and immediately took off his cloak and gave it to the man."[28] Compassion toward those who could be of no use to him was not a component of Francis's persona as the son of a capitalist (although later biographies gloss over his youth to make him appear saintly from the start). It was a trait that had been repressed in the course of adaptation. Giotto's painting uses the medieval device of compressing time by depicting consecutive events within one pictorial frame to visually suggest that the compassion actualized in the incident with the cloak was always present in him. Francis's impending inner transformation is already visually anticipated by his halo. This medieval artistic device mirrors Jung's understanding of individuation as the unfolding in time of an archetypal potential. Francis's capacity for compassion, while not a part of his conscious persona, is already contained in the spiritually holy, psychologically whole person he is destined to become. Giving away his cloak, which is part of his persona identity, is the first step.

The next fresco in the series shows the dream that signaled the beginning of Francis's struggle to differentiate between his persona and his ego, a critical stage in the process of individuation. According to Whitmont, the persona "appears in dreams as the images of clothes, uniforms, and masks."[29] Francis's persona was represented in his dream through the physical trappings of knighthood.

Bonaventure's inscription says, "Francis had a dream one night in which he saw a splendid and sumptuous palace equipped with knightly armoury, and with weapons embellished with the sign of the cross of Christ. When Francis asked to whom all this belonged, he received the reply from on high: that it would all belong to him and his knights."[30] In Giotto's painting, Christ, standing behind the sleeping Francis, directs our attention to the palace. On the roof over the entrance are four knightly tunics emblazoned with red crosses. Hanging from the upper windows and inside the upper rooms are banners and flags and armor, all decorated with crosses of gold. Francis saw this palace in his dream, and, encouraged by the impending glory he anticipated, he set out for Spoleto, the first stop on his journey to meet the crusaders in Apulia. But in Spoleto he had another dream. In this dream a voice spoke to him. Fortini, using material from the thirteenth-century *Legend of the Three Companions,* recreates what Francis heard in his dream. First, the voice asked, "Who do you think can best reward you, the servant or the Master?" When Francis responded that it would be the Master, the voice went on to ask, "Then why do you leave the Master for the servant, the rich Lord for the poor man?" When Francis realized that he had misinterpreted the meaning of his previous dream, he did not know how to proceed. Then the voice told him, "Return to your own place and you will be told what to do."[31]

Francis's dreams were introducing him to the paradoxical nature of reality. What appeared most valuable—glory and wealth—would not serve him as well as their opposites—humility and poverty. Francis returned to Assisi. He did not yet know who the Master was or how he was to serve him, but he was compelled, against all dominant social values, to give up his dream of becoming the knight his father and Assisi expected him to be. Francis had embarked on the process of individuation, a process that would turn him into a knight fighting for Christ's peace outfitted in an armor of poverty.

Francis did not shed his old persona right away. Celano describes the process of transforming the persona values of merchant's son and aspiring knight into values in tune with Francis's authentic personality and vocation. He stresses the movement from secular to spiritual values: "He withdrew for a while from the bustle and the business of the world and tried to establish Jesus Christ dwelling within himself. Like a prudent business man, he hid the treasure he had found from the eyes of the deluded, and having sold all his possessions, he tried to buy it secretly."[32] Francis operated "like a prudent business man." He did not announce what he was beginning to discover until he understood its worth. This new knowledge was something he must buy once he discovered its price. His mind, as presented by Celano, still thought in terms of value and exchange; however, the object of value and the medium of exchange had changed.

That Francis still thought like a merchant's son attests to the authenticity of his individuation journey. He could not eliminate the values his father had instilled any more than we can undo the person we became as a result of our childhood training. What he needed to do was to transform those values to serve his own needs. Francis understood that he must withdraw from the world to understand this new form of commerce. His previous withdrawals had been involuntary. He had been imprisoned and then ill. *This* withdrawal was by choice. He had to become acquainted with what Jung called "the God within," and what Daryl Sharp, in his Jungian lexicon, defines as "the archetype of wholeness and the regulating center of the psyche; a transpersonal power that transcends the ego."[33]

This archetype had to be accessed to provide a direction for a life that differed from collective values.

Francis possessed intuitive psychological wisdom about this new inner journey. He knew that confronting God was a dangerous business and that he would need a companion to both ground him and witness his journey. Just as a modern person who has embarked on the psycho-spiritual process of individuation does well to choose a friend or wise mentor to assist with the journey, Francis always had a companion nearby to support him after his encounters with the divine. Celano describes the first of these relationships: "There was a certain man in the city of Assisi whom he loved more than any other because he was of the same age as the other, and since the great familiarity of their mutual affection led him to share his secrets with him, he often took him to remote places, places well-suited for counsel, telling him that he had found a certain great and precious treasure."[34] Francis's friend would stay outside the caves on Mt. Subasio above Assisi where Francis went to pray, and he was there to support him "when he came out again to his companion,...so exhausted with the strain, that one person seemed to have entered and another to have come out."[35] Finally, after a long struggle, Francis discovered what he needed to do. The merchant's son had to sell all that he had.

Francis set off for nearby Foligno, where "he sold everything he had with him, and, successful as a merchant, he left behind even the horse he was riding, after he had received payment for it."[36] Francis, again thinking like a merchant who can solve his problems by throwing money at them, attempted to give this money to a poor priest and asked to use the priest's church, San Damiano, as a place of refuge.

To this point, Francis's actions had been those of a man who thinks in terms of money. The priest, skeptical about the depth of Francis's transformation, refused to keep the money because, according to Celano, "he had seen him just the day before...in a riotous way...and showing greater foolishness than the rest."[37] Perhaps the priest intuitively realized that Francis had not yet separated himself from his former values but was just reacting to them, or maybe he was afraid of taking the money from the son of Pietro Bernardone. However, he did allow Francis to hide from his father in a pit. And this pit, like the caves on Mt. Subasio, became a container for Francis's transformation.

Jungian psychology posits the need for sacred space for inner transformation. This space, sometimes referred to as the womb of the tomb, is the place where the old persona can die and the ego can become enlarged and strengthened enough to deal with both the personal and the collective unconscious. It is a place of death and rebirth before moving out again into the world. Throughout his life, Frances would alternate between places of solitude and spiritual rebirth and the demands of the world of action. His time at San Damiano established this pattern. After a month spent hiding out in the pit, he had gained sufficient ego strength to emerge and confront his father.

When Francis walked back up to Assisi from San Damiano below the city, he was transformed. The merchant's son was penniless, emaciated, and shabby; and the former aspiring knight was now "bearing the shield of faith to fight for the Lord, armed with great confidence."[38] Francis could no longer conceal this transformation. His old persona was gone. He was no longer operating under collective values.

The reaction of the people of Assisi was to turn against him. "Shouting out that he was mad and demented, they threw the mud of the street and stones at him."[39] Francis's father imprisoned him in his house and tried to beat him into submission.

Francis's mother reacted differently, however. She had a sense of herself that was differentiated from her persona role as the wife of Pietro Bernardone. According to Celano, she "did not approve of what her husband had done."[40] So while her husband was away on business, "when she saw that he [Francis] could not be persuaded away from his purpose, she was moved by motherly compassion for him, and loosening his chains, she let him go free."[41] "Motherly compassion" is an empathetic reaction that will later direct Francis in his relationship with the brothers of the order he will found. It is, according to Sharp, "based on the unconscious projection of subjective contents."[42] Because Francis's mother needed to honor her own unique spirituality, she projected this need on her son and honored it in him. This is the same unconscious projection that moved her to name him for John the Baptist. Jung describes such empathy by saying, "The man with the empathetic attitude finds himself...in a world that needs his subjective feeling to give it life and soul. He animates it with himself."[43] Just as his mother projects her own spiritual values onto Francis and in rescuing him partially rescues some essential reality about herself, Francis will animate the whole world with his developing spirituality, a process that will culminate at the end of his life in the *Canticle of Brother Sun,* discussed in chapter 8.

Earlier in his life, Francis was rescued from prison by his father. Later he was rescued by his mother from his father. But now he no longer needs rescuing. He has found a purpose to life that makes him immune to external danger. Celano describes the meeting between Francis and his father to show that Francis is no longer bound by his father's values: "When this child of grace heard his carnally minded father coming to him, confident and joyful he went to meet him, exclaiming in a clear voice that he cared nothing for his chains and blows. Moreover he stated that he would gladly undergo evils for the name of Christ."[44] Francis is now a "child of grace," whereas his father is "carnally minded." Francis is "confident and joyful," far different from the young man who spent a month cowering in a pit to avoid confronting his father. Francis has learned the mystery of undergoing the process of individuation. He has learned to suffer the pain and confusion of life and has been transformed by this process. He has undergone what St. John of the Cross called "the dark night of the soul"[45] and has emerged a new man.

Jung asserts the reality of this experience, even though it is inaccessible to empirical measurement: "Rebirth is not a process that we can in any way observe. We can neither measure nor weigh nor photograph it. It is entirely beyond sense perception....One speaks of rebirth; one professes rebirth; one is filled with rebirth....We have to be content with its psychic reality."[46]

The psycho-spiritual reality of Francis's rebirth was manifested in a dramatic moment in front of Santa Maria Maggiore, Assisi's cathedral at that time. The bishop publicly presented Pietro's claim in front of the cathedral.[47] Standing before his father, the citizens of his town, and his bishop, representatives of all the collective values that had shaped his previous adaptation to life, Francis stripped himself naked and returned both his father's money and all of his clothes. Giotto depicts this scene in the basilica in Assisi. Francis, his lower body covered by the bishop's cloak, has his arms and eyes raised to heaven. God's hand blesses him from the sky. Across the way, Pietro, holding Francis's clothes, is restrained from striking him by a citizen of Assisi. Meanwhile two children, holding a supply of rocks they brought to throw at Francis, solemnly discuss this new turn of events. Bonaventure's inscription reads, "Francis gave back everything to his father even the clothes

Saint Francis Gives His Clothes to His Father by Giotto di Bondone
(S. Francesco, Assisi, Italy).

he was wearing, renounced his right of inheritance and said to his father: 'Henceforth with all certainty I can say Our Father who art in heaven because Peter Bernardone has repudiated me.'"[48]

Francis's rebirth has given him a new father, and his radical repudiation of worldly values has introduced a new value that causes the citizens of Assisi to relent in their persecution. What had appeared to be worthless nonconformity was now beginning to open up new possibilities in the collective realm. Whitmont's description of self-actualization during the process of individuation is relevant to understanding the impact of Francis's public declaration and its acceptance by the people of Assisi: "Our collective morality is challenged by what presents itself as individual conscience and as the meaning of a uniquely appointed life."[49] Challenged by the authenticity of Francis's reaction to his father, the children in Giotto's fresco leave their rocks unthrown.

Despite his transformation, Francis maintained the essential core of his personality. He was still the merchant's son who made his break with the old life in terms of money and clothes, and he was still the dramatic actor who once led the *Tripundanti* to commemorate sacred and secular events, but he was now dramatizing the change in his own life before all of Assisi. What had changed was Francis's relationship to his old way of thinking and behaving. His persona, which used to be a mask that covered his essential nature, was now a vehicle for expressing his relationship to the Self that Jung calls "the God within." Now the cloth merchant's son uses nakedness to dramatize his new relationship with God.

One other detail in this public expression of rebirth is important to note. Although Francis has returned his clothes, and with them his old persona, he is not entirely naked. He is partially covered by the cloak of Bishop Guido, a representative of the church. Francis's psycho-spiritual journey is in some ways captured by this image. For although Celano's first biography sums up this incident by saying that "only the wall of flesh should separate him from the vision of God,"[50] the image of the cloak remains. Not until he is nearing death and asks his brothers to lay him naked on the ground, will the cloak of the church be finally removed and, symbolically, the psycho-spiritual journey completed.

CHAPTER FOUR
Looking at the Shadow

The process of individuation requires a relationship with the *shadow,* what Sharp calls the "hidden or unconscious aspects of oneself, both good and bad, which the ego has either repressed or never recognized."[51] The shadow is projected onto someone else rather than being recognized as one's own hidden nature, because it is at odds with the persona. When the ego is identified with the persona, it cannot accept the legitimacy of the shadow. We can learn to recognize our shadow, however, if we are willing to accept that we are not the person we think we are. All we need do is to consider the people and characteristics that trigger a powerful repugnance in us. When someone really "gets our goat," we are *scapegoating* that person as our shadow.

The notion of scapegoating is one window into the mechanism of shadow projection. In ancient times, a goat was literally sacrificed to propitiate the gods. The gods were "out there" and the goat was "out there" and the action of making things right was "out there." None of the guilt for wrongdoing had to be internalized. The whole process of recognizing that a wrong had been done and of righting that wrong was ritually handled through animal sacrifice.[52] However, as guilt became internalized and animal sacrifice disappeared, scapegoating became less conscious.

Scapegoating, whether conscious or unconscious, has

always had a collective as well as a personal dimension. Just as an individual projects what is unacceptable onto others rather than accepting it as part of the total personality, society scapegoats what is unacceptable and tries to sacrifice it in the interest of the conscious social ideal. The violence of the twelfth and thirteenth centuries attests to the prevalence of scapegoating. Moslems and Jews were scapegoated as the infidel. It was simpler to go on a crusade and kill some "heathens" than to address the worldliness of Christians at home. Crusaders in the East visited barbaric violence upon Moslems and Jews in Jerusalem, a violence that spilled over, during the Fourth Crusade of Francis's youth, to the Christian cities of Zara and Constantinople. Some would say this scapegoating mechanism was at work during the Vietnam and Gulf wars. Rather than confronting our domestic problems in all their complexity, we fought the enemy far away who looked and talked and acted differently than we did. Meanwhile, just as in the thirteenth century, our own problems multiplied.

Scapegoating occurs in politics as well. The history of the struggle between the Guelphs and the Ghibellines in Francis's Italy is a study in the need to project confusion and anxiety about social change onto another political group. They become the destroyers of the social order who must be vanquished at all cost. The thirteenth century was a transitional time between feudalism and medieval Christianity on the one hand, and secular humanism on the other. The new values of the rising bourgeoisie, supported by papal power, were pitted against the traditional values of the nobility, supported by the emperor. Both sides operated with tunnel vision, labeling the other as the evil ones. That way they did not have to struggle with the complexity and moral ambiguity inherent in change.

The thirteenth century was also similar to our own times

in its projection of anxiety about the human condition onto human physicality. Just as we swarm to fitness centers to punish our bodies for their excess flesh and become bulimic or anorexic to deny the reality of our physicality, crowds of medieval penitents traveled through towns scourging themselves in atonement for their evil physicality. A scapegoating of human physicality and the material world was also expressed in the Albigensian heresy, which posited a dualistic universe. The material world, ruled by an evil god, was in conflict with the spiritual world, ruled by a benign divinity. Medieval Christianity contained a very ambiguous message about the human body. The regulation of priestly celibacy and the adulation of the Virgin were two manifestations of this uneasiness about sexuality. However, rather than working through this ambivalence and accepting moral ambiguity, the church exterminated the Cathars and with them any real consideration of spirit in matter.

Lepers, like victims of AIDS today, were also convenient scapegoats for anxiety about physicality and the complexity of human contact. It was easier to ostracize lepers than to identify with their plight and attempt to help them. Francis's first recognition of his personal shadow occurred when he embraced a leper. To understand why a leper might receive Francis's projected shadow, it is necessary to consider his conscious persona. Francis identified with the person his father and the citizens of Assisi expected him to be. Rich and well dressed, popular and funloving, he had a clearly defined role within the life of the city. His prospects were promising. He was the very opposite of the lepers who lived in isolation outside the city walls. Poor and horribly deformed, they were legal and religious outcasts, separated by formal ritual from the rest of society.[53] All they could anticipate was a grim life ended by a lonely death.

Francis was appalled by lepers and went out of his way to

avoid any contact with them. In *The First Life of Saint Francis,* Celano recollects Francis saying that "he would look at their houses only from a distance of two miles and he would hold his nostrils with his hands."[54] The vehemence of his reaction to lepers suggests that they carried his shadow. In *The Second life of Francis,* Celano says, "For among all the unhappy spectacles of the world Francis naturally abhorred lepers."[55] Celano considered his abhorrence "natural" because it accorded with the collective values of the day, values that allowed people to dismiss lepers as members of the human family. It was also psychologically natural for a man who identified with a socially acceptable persona to project the repressed contents of his unconscious onto society's least acceptable members.

The vehemence of Francis's loathing of lepers also suggests that his repression of compassion in order to maintain the persona of the merchant's son cost him a great deal in terms of psychic energy. Jung explains that the greatest amount of negative *affects* are usually activated "where adaptation is weakest, and at the same time they reveal the reason for the weakness, namely a certain degree of inferiority and the existence of a lower level of personality...singularly incapable of moral judgment."[56] Because Francis's adaptation to the callous attitude of his society violated his authentic personality, he was "singularly incapable of moral judgment" in his dealings with lepers. His authentic compassion was repressed and stunted by adaptation, so it expressed itself in horror instead of empathy.

Jung called the shadow "a moral problem that challenges the whole ego-personality."[57] Francis perceived his problem with lepers in the same way. In the *Testament,* which he wrote during his final illness, he credits his confrontation with the moral problem of his attitude toward lepers as critical to his transformation:

This is how God inspired me, Brother Francis, to embark upon a life of penance. When I was in sin, the sight of lepers nauseated me beyond measure; but then God himself led me into their company, and I had pity on them. When I had once become acquainted with them, what had previously nauseated me became a source of spiritual and physical consolation for me. After that I did not wait long before leaving the world.[58]

In psychological language, being "in sin" means being identified with his collective persona and estranged from his authentic personality. When Francis reached out to a leper in compassion, he established a relationship with his own shadow and was healed of that rift. What had previously nauseated him was now "a source of spiritual and physical consolation."

Celano dramatizes Francis's transforming encounter with a leper:

One day he met a leper while he was riding near Assisi. Though the leper caused him no small disgust and horror, nevertheless, lest like a transgressor of a commandment he should break his given word, he got off his horse and prepared to kiss the leper. But when the leper put out his hand as though to receive something, he received money along with a kiss. And immediately mounting his horse, Francis looked here and there about him; but though the plain lay clear and open on all sides, and there were no obstacles about, he could not see the leper anywhere.[59]

Celano compares Francis's situation, were he to avoid the moral problem of embracing the leper, to that of "a transgressor of a commandment." Francis is operating under a higher morality now than the collective mores of his society. As Jung noted, there is a moral problem involved in dealing with the shadow. In Celano's account,

Francis also experiences the challenge to his ego-personality that Jung observed. The leper reaches out his hand expecting alms. Francis, the merchant's son, accustomed to throwing money at his problems, accompanies the money with a kiss. This action enlarges his conscious personality by adding compassion to the generosity that characterized his former prodigality and puts him in touch, both physically and psychologically, with his shadow.

The end of the story is interesting from the standpoint of individuation. After Francis kisses the leper, the leper disappears. There is no rational explanation for his disappearance. Celano stresses that the landscape was clear all around. In psychological terms, the leper has disappeared because Francis has brought his shadow into the light of consciousness. There is no one there but Francis.

After Francis established a relationship with his shadow, it no longer frightened him. Throughout his life he worked with lepers and used their companionship to ground himself when he feared that his ego might become inflated as a result of a particularly numinous experience. By seeing *himself* in lepers, he discriminated between his ego and his God and avoided being consumed by his mystical experiences. His shadow protected him from too much light.

Francis became conscious, after a moral struggle, of his shadow projected onto lepers. However, after he discarded his persona of the merchant's son and was able to accept his own psychological leper, he projected his shadow onto his own physicality. It took Francis the rest of his life to withdraw that projection, which was the shadow side of his former persona. The early Francis was a carousing dandy who roamed the streets of Assisi singing the love songs of the troubadours and who lived according to the reality of the sensual world. The shadow of this Francis was an ascetic mystic who experienced his own physical reality as an impediment to direct experience of his God. When he discarded his former persona, Francis projected his shadow onto the body that had expressed his former personality and adopted instead the persona of the ascetic. Because his own body was carrying his shadow, it was impossible for Francis to see the projection.

Jung discusses the difficulty of consciously integrating all aspects of the shadow:

> Although with insight and good will, the shadow can to some extent be assimilated into the conscious personality, experience shows that there are certain features which offer the most obstinate resistance to moral control and prove almost impossible to influence. These resistances are usually bound up with projections that are not recognized as such, and their recognition is a moral achievement beyond the ordinary.[60]

Francis could not see that he had projected his shadow onto his body. His blindness in regard to his body was noted by Celano as the only area in which Francis's words differed from his actions. Francis taught that "Brother body should be provided for with discretion, so that a tempest of bad temper be not raised by it."[61] For others, he pragmatically recognized that excessive mortification of the body increased, rather than decreased, interference with spiritual concentration. However, he disregarded this advice when it came to his own body: "For he subjected his own innocent body to scourgings and want, multiplying its *wounds without cause.*"[62] Celano refers to Francis's body as "innocent" and calls his excessive mortification "without cause." While Francis's chronic ill health attests to the practical validity of Celano's complaint, Celano's reservation about Francis's extreme asceticism is particularly compelling because it is his only criticism of Francis's life. Even

Celano, writing within the uncritical genre of hagiography, had to note Francis's extreme alienation from his own body. It was not until the end of Francis's life, when, according to tradition, his body had become the medium for receiving the wounds of Christ, that he could apologize to "Brother Donkey," his body, for all the indignities it had been forced to undergo.

Francis punished his body for its potential sinfulness. One way that he believed his body could trick him into sin was through lust. Fearing betrayal of his spirituality by his body, he projected his shadow onto women as well as onto his own physicality. His fear of contact with women, with the exception of those who will be discussed in chapter 5 below, which explores his anima, suggests a weak adaptation to celibacy resulting in a primitive reaction against women.

In *The Second Life of Saint Francis,* Celano calls contact with women "honeyed poison" which "leads astray even holy men" and goes on to say, "Indeed, a woman was so unwelcome to him that you would think his caution was not a warning or an example but rather a dread or a horror."[63] Celano's phrase "honeyed poison" suggests Francis's ambivalence about women. Their powerful attraction is experienced as being toxic. Celano recognizes the extreme *affect,* "a dread or a horror," that women have on Francis. The language Celano uses, though suggestive of his own misogyny, also suggests that women do not exist for Francis apart from the contamination of the repressed sexuality of his own projected shadow. His inability to see this projection is also suggested by Celano when he quotes Francis as saying, "I would not recognize any woman if I looked into her face, except two [whose identities will be explored in a later chapter]. The face of the one and the other is known to me, but I know no other."[64] Francis is literally unable to look at women because he will see his own shadow if he does.

Another clue that women *constellate* the shadow for Francis comes from the rigidity and dismissiveness of his attitude. Celano quotes Francis as saying, "What business should a Friar Minor have to transact with a woman, except when she piously asks for holy penance or for advice concerning a better life."[65] Even in this exemplary business, Francis was hesitant to deal with women. He established a Second Order of religious women (his friars being the First Order), but he so rarely visited them that "at times the brothers wondered that Francis did not visit the holy servants of Christ with his corporal presence more often."[66] On one occasion, when he finally relented and the nuns assembled at San Damiano for a sermon, Francis made a circle of ashes around himself and sprinkled the rest of the ashes on his head. He then stood in silence in the middle of the circle. Evidently the nuns got the message, for Celano reports in *The Second Life of St. Francis* that "their tears flowed in abundance and they could scarcely restrain their hands from inflicting punishment on themselves."[67] The nuns internalized Francis's projection and experienced his loathing of their physicality. Celano summarizes the sermon: "By his actions he taught them that they should regard themselves as ashes and that there was nothing in his heart concerning them but what was fitting this consideration."[68] Francis's inability to see his shadow projected onto his own physicality and onto women was damaging to his body and his psyche and to the bodies and psyches of the women who followed him.

Francis's blindness to his shadow when it was projected onto women was symptomatic of the collective unconscious of the thirteenth century. As Jung observed, the shadow can have both positive and negative components. Women carried both. Peterson, a biographer of St. Clare, discusses the opposing images of women in the medieval psyche:

"Medieval women were confronted with mixed messages. Women are good [the message of chivalry and courtly love]. [But] women are bad. Women make men do bad things." This negative message came from both the Roman and the Judeo-Christian legacy. "Because of women, men do good things." Chivalry and courtly love supported this idea. "The standard preaching was that women's bodies were sources of sin for men."[69] Because the evil aspect of the feminine was rooted in her sexuality, accessing the good required overcoming that sexuality. Therefore, according to Peterson, "The finest thing that a woman could do to be considered clean was to make a vow of virginity, and then she would not be responsible for the evil things that women did to men."[70]

The archetypal virgin was, of course, the Virgin Mary. According to Christian theology, "Sin came through a woman [Eve], but salvation through a virgin. The solution was to hate women but love virgins."[71] It is no coincidence that the twelfth and thirteenth centuries saw the creation of the Gothic cathedral that, like the Virgin to whom it was dedicated, seemed to transcend its own physical limitations as it rose above the earth, transforming matter into spiritual light.

However, the thirteenth-century psyche also had a special reverence for Mary Magdalene, because it projected onto her both woman's evil sexuality and its redemption through renunciation. According to Peterson, "Mary Magdalene was one of the best-loved female saints, for she combined both sides of women's nature. As a public sinner, Mary Magdalene stood as public evidence of the misogynist view of women; as a penitent, she became a saint."[72] Francis's personal shadow contained the mixture of misogyny and reverence that the collective unconscious projected onto medieval women. He feared women as a source of temptation and corruption. However, as we have already indicated, there were two women in his outer life whom he loved and admired, whose faces he knew. His inner life also contained two important women who could serve as his spiritual guides. These women, discussed in the next chapter, put him in touch with the feminine side of his nature.

In addition to struggling with society's ambivalence toward women, Francis had to come to terms with the collective violence of the thirteenth century. He had to discern the authentic reaction of his total personality to the collective scapegoating of his times. Having relinquished his collectively determined persona and integrated part of his shadow into ego consciousness, Francis was able to access what John Sanford calls "the ethic of creativity." This ethic is the opposite of the "ethic of obedience" to collective morality. Fritz Kunkel describes the creativity of authentic discernment as "traveling without a map and without security."[73] Francis demonstrated creative solutions to collective projections on numerous occasions.

One of the most famous of these occasions comes from the fourteenth-century *Fioretti,* a collection of stories about Francis that includes additions to thirteenth-century accounts. According to the legend, a ferocious wolf was terrorizing the people of the Italian hill town of Gubbio. Read psychologically, the wolf is the shadow of civilized behavior; it is violent instinctuality that threatens to devour rational order. The people of Gubbio experienced the wolf as a dangerous enemy and attempted to deal with it collectively through violence: "All men went armed when they went forth from the city as if they were going to battle; and therewithal they were not able to defend themselves from him, when haply any man encountered him alone."[74] Francis, on the contrary, encountered the wolf alone, "putting all his trust in God"[75] rather than in collective violence. When commanded "in Christ's name," the wolf "came, gentle as a lamb, and laid himself down at the feet of Saint Francis."[76]

Francis communicates with the opposite side of the wolf's nature, which is "gentle as a lamb." However, Francis does not have a sentimental view of the wolf's potential peacefulness. He intuitively understands what Jung calls *compensation* and Sharp defines as "a natural process aimed at establishing or maintaining balance within the psyche."[77] If the wolf is to manifest its lamb side to the people of Gubbio, its wolf side must be consciously accommodated. First Francis acknowledges his connection to the wolf by calling it his brother, "friar wolf."[78] He then catalogues all the damage the wolf has done and presents him with a fitting punishment according to collective morality: "Thou dost merit the gallows as a thief and most ubiquitous murderer; and all men cry out against thee."[79] However Francis, inspired by the ethic of creativity rather than collective morality, seeks a solution that will benefit both parties. He couches his proposal in such a way that the solution will appeal to the self-interest of the wolf; it will compensate his violent nature for behaving like a lamb: "I desire, friar wolf, to make peace between thee and them; to the end that thou mayest no more offend them and that they may forgive thee all thy past offences and neither men nor dogs may pursue thee any more."[80]

Francis's proposal of peace will gain the wolf both forgiveness and a cessation of hostility. It will remedy the damage that has been caused. However, compensation requires more than a clean slate. If peace is to endure, the cause of hostility must be eliminated. Francis includes this root cause in his proposal to wolf and townspeople. Once the wolf signals its acceptance of the concept of peace "by movements of his body and tail and eyes, and by bowing his head,"[81] Francis explains how the peace can be kept: "Friar wolf, inasmuch as it seemeth good unto thee to make and keep this peace, I promise thee that, so long as thou shalt live, I will cause thy food to be given thee continuously by the men of this city, so that thou shalt no more suffer hunger; for I know full well that whatever of evil thou hast done, thou hast done it through hunger."[82]

The townspeople will feed the wolf, and the wolf will agree to keep its rapacious appetites in check. Francis understands that if the instinctual side of nature is starved, it will turn dangerous. If nourished, like a gentle lamb it can coexist in harmony with the rest of life. Francis and the wolf shake hand to paw, a symbol of a peaceful relationship between the conscious ego and the shadow.

Then, to transform the collective consciousness as well, Francis has the covenant witnessed in the central piazza: "All the people with one voice promised to provide him food continually...and the wolf...showed as far as he was able his determination to keep that covenant wholly."[83] So profound was the peace created through this pact that the wolf roamed the town freely for the rest of its life, and "never did any dog bark after him."[84] Total psychological integration is suggested by the harmony among townspeople, domestic animals, and a savage beast.

Another famous example of Francis's ability to befriend the collective shadow occurred during the crusade against Damietta in 1219. Here Francis met with the sultan in an attempt to convert him. As in the incident with the wolf of Gubbio, Francis substitutes negotiation for violence, "preaching where the sword had failed."[85] Although it was beyond his power to effect a lasting peace as he did in Gubbio, Francis did manage to creatively interact with the sultan outside the violent paradigm of the Crusades. Giotto depicts Francis's encounter with the sultan in terms of fire,

Test of Fire before the Sultan by the School of Giotto di Bondone
(S. Francesco, Assisi, Italy).

a symbol of transformation. Although Celano describes the encounter with the sultan in *The First Life of Saint Francis*, it is Bonaventure who introduces the psychologically powerful image of fire. In his inscription below Giotto's fresco in the basilica, Bonaventure says, "In testimony to the truth of the faith of Christ, Francis challenged the priests of the sultan of Babylonia to walk through fire with him. But none of them was willing to accept the challenge; they all fled immediately from the presence of Francis and the sultan."[86] In the painting, the sultan points to Francis; Francis's extended arm continues the gesture to the fire, linking the enemy of Christianity, the proponent of Christianity, and the transforming fire. Giotto later treats the same theme in Santa Croce. In the later fresco, the fire is between the two men, suggesting even more powerfully the transformative power of the fire of love to dispel the shadows we project upon each other.

CHAPTER FIVE
Feminine Energy

Francis experienced people, animals, and even inanimate objects with empathy. Except where his projected shadow blocked his vision, he delighted in God's immanence in every aspect of creation. This chapter will explore Francis's capacity for joy and connectedness in the context of Jung's discoveries about the *anima,* the feminine psychological energy available to men.

The idea that there is feminine and masculine energy is very old. Chinese philosophy posits yin and yang, yin being the dark, passive, feminine energy of the earth and yang the light, active, masculine energy of heaven. Without their opposition and interaction, there can be no life or movement. Western culture tends to emphasize yang energy and ignore the feminine yin energy. Only in the Virgin is there recognition of the critical role of the feminine in giving birth to the light of the world.

Because of the emphasis on masculine energy in the Judeo-Christian tradition, there has been a militant, extraverted, misogynist quality to Western culture. Jung believed that one of a man's individuation tasks was to become conscious of his feminine energy, which in religious language is called his *soul.* But before that can happen, a man gets to know his anima by projecting it onto women in the outer world.

Francis's first experience of his anima came through his

mother. Jung called this the *Eve stage* of anima relationship. During this stage, the feminine can only be accessed through a personal relationship. This stage is critical because, as Whitmont explains, "Whoever incorporates the feminine image most decisively for the child provokes the pattern in terms of which the anima is actualized into the personal realm."[87] Francis's mother provided an important part of the pattern for anima actualization.

Francis's mother, Lady Pica, was probably from Provençe, an area of both troubadours and the Albigensian heresy. Through his mother, Francis came to know the ideals of courtly love and chivalric courtesy. His spiritual quest was couched in the language of courtly love and imbued with the courtesy of his mother's people.

Through Lady Pica, Francis may also have been exposed to the Cathars' belief that the good God was totally absent from the physical world. While Francis never, except during his depression, lost consciousness of God's immanence in creation, his excessive asceticism may have been influenced by Cathar spirituality.

Francis also experienced through his mother the courage to confront social authority. It was Lady Pica who defied the authority of her husband by releasing Francis from the family cellar and who, according to Celano's *The First Life of Saint Francis,* received her husband's wrath when "not finding Francis, he turned to upbraid his wife, heaping sins upon sins."[88]

So by the time Francis confronted his father in front of Bishop Guido, Lady Pica had constellated his anima in the outer world. Her complex French heritage from the troubadours and Cathars, her intuitive spirituality that united him in a special way to Christ, and her moral courage and compassion were juxtaposed to his father's masculine persona, which defined itself in terms of pragmatic capitalism and a violent reaction to opposition. However, Lady Pica was not able to actualize Francis's whole anima. As Whitmont explains, "Since the anima represents the Eternal Feminine in its widest potentialities, its arch core contains much more than can ever be constellated by the actual mother."[89] Francis needed other women to help him become conscious of the feminine side of his nature.

Two other women, Clare of Assisi and Lady Jacoba of Rome, assisted Francis in getting to know his anima through the mechanism of projection, whereby he saw his own feminine aspect reflected in the outer world. Both Clare and Lady Jacoba were of the noble class, which separated them from his father's values. Virginity and widowhood rescued them from the taint of sexuality. Francis could safely look into their faces to see his projected anima without fearing the corruption of money or sex.

Clare, born to the noble Offreduccio family in 1194, was twelve years younger than Francis. Like Francis, she was raised in the midst of political violence. Francis's family, as members of the merchant class, fought against the Offreduccios and the other nobility of Assisi. When Clare was five years old, the Rocca was razed and her house destroyed by citizens from Francis's class. Her family had to go into exile in Perugia. Francis himself may have participated in the destruction of Clare's life in Assisi.

Perugia's protection of Assisi's exiled nobility re-ignited the traditional hostility between the two cities. Supported by Perugia's nobility, the exiles from Assisi fought for reinstatement and reparation. In 1201 at the Battle of Collestrada, the noble forces defeated the knights of the commune. Francis was imprisoned. Eventually, a shaky peace was established between the two cities and within Assisi. Francis was ransomed by his father, and Clare returned home. The wealthy merchants rebuilt what they had destroyed in return for political control. It was in this context of violence and clashing interests that Francis's relationship with Clare unfolded.

In Clare, Francis could see the contemplative dimension of his own spirituality. Clare came from a family of deeply spiritual women. Her childhood was defined by their rich prayer life and their acts of compassion in Assisi. Yet Clare, like Francis, had to struggle against her society's attempt to define her. While Francis's persona was largely defined by his membership in the merchant class, Clare's identity was most importantly defined by her sexual status. Thirteenth-century women were virgins, married women, or widows. Virgins and widows had the most autonomy. Like many women in the twelfth and thirteenth centuries, Clare took a vow of virginity. She also sold her dowry to make herself undesirable for marriage. Although Clare's male relatives intended that she should marry, Clare was determined to maintain her spiritual freedom. Her initial struggle was with her male relatives. Her lifelong struggle was with a male ecclesiastical hierarchy that could not understand or honor her spiritual need for absolute poverty.

Clare left her aristocratic life behind her in a manner that was just as dramatic as Francis's renunciation of his capitalistic origins. On the night after Palm Sunday in 1212, she crept out of her family's home in the middle of the night. She left through the "death door," a special opening used only for removing a coffin from the house. Her departure through this door signaled her death to her former life. Clare walked through the night to a tiny church below Assisi, one of the churches Francis had repaired when the cross spoke to him. There Francis gave her a tonsure. The tonsure was a visible sign of her inner conversion and guaranteed her status as a virgin. No man would have her now.

Just as Francis suffered violence from Pietro Bernardone,

Clare was accosted by her uncle (her father being dead), who tried to force her to return home. But whereas Francis had to spend a month in the pit at San Damiano before summoning the courage to confront his father, Clare was able to confront her uncle the day after she fled to Francis. She intuitively deflected her uncle's violence by meeting him at the altar of a church, where she unveiled her tonsured head. What Francis had to agonize over, Clare did instinctively.

Francis grew to an understanding of his own spirituality partly by projecting his own spiritual attributes onto Clare. Whitmont explains that "because the anima cannot be perceived directly, inner expectations, hopes, and fears will automatically be projected."[90] In the calm, contemplative life at San Damiano, Francis could see his own spiritual aspirations being realized. And in Clare's struggle for ecclesiastical approval of "the privilege of poverty," a new, radical definition of institutional as well as individual poverty for her sisters at San Damiano, Francis could recognize his own fear for the integrity of Lady Poverty within the framework of the church. In the midst of his own active life, Francis could project his own anima energy onto Clare, cloistered at San Damiano.

This projection of anima energy can be extremely dangerous to a woman as she travels along her own psycho-spiritual journey. The previous chapter described the reaction of the Poor Clares to Francis's sermon of ashes, in which the projection of his shadow constellated their own feelings of worthlessness. Whitmont articulates this danger: "The man's anima projection always offers a great temptation to the woman. She will tend to identify with his expectations....[This identification] may make her lose her own soul, her own real identity, in the process."[91] Fortunately for both Francis and Clare, Clare's spiritual identity was firmly established before she ever joined him. She saw her own authentic spirituality

mirrored in the life of Francis. As Francis translated his contemplative spirituality into the world of action, he could rely
on Clare to maintain a spiritual center of strength within the
contemplative life at San Damiano.

In *The First Life of Saint Francis,* Celano enumerates the
virtues of the Second Order that Francis established at San
Damiano under the leadership of Clare. This list gives
insight into Francis's own feminine nature as it was mirrored by Clare. The virtues are charity, humility, virginity
and chastity, poverty, abstinence and silence, patience, and
contemplation.[92] The virtues that were lived in the cloistered world of San Damiano were the virtues Francis tried
to expand into the secular world of the thirteenth century.

While Francis saw in Clare his own projected virtues and
spiritual strengths that he went on to actualize in his own life
and in the lives of those in his orders, it was onto Lady Jacoba
that he projected the more earthy aspects of his anima. Lady
Jacoba was a Roman widow of a noble family. The role of
widows who chose celibacy for the remainder of their lives
was highly valued in the early church, and surfaced again in
the twelfth and thirteenth centuries. A life of celibacy
removed a woman from the perceived evil of her sexuality.

Lady Jacoba belonged to the Third Order of Franciscans,
one of the first lay orders formally recognized by the
church, which was founded by Francis around 1210. Francis stayed with Lady Jacoba whenever he was in Rome and
relied on her for the creature comforts and human companionship that he normally would not allow himself. In his
Treatise on the Miracles of the Blessed Francis, Celano attests to
the unique place Lady Jacoba occupied in Francis's world.
When Francis lay dying, he sent a messenger to Rome to
fetch Lady Jacoba. While the messenger was getting ready
to leave, Lady Jacoba arrived. Francis's response to news of
her arrival was "Blessed be God who has guided the Lady

Jacoba, our brother, to us. Open the door and bring her in, for our Brother Jacoba does not have to observe the decree against women."[93]

Francis considered Lady Jacoba a "brother." While he never forgot that women were somewhat dangerous, Lady Jacoba was outside "the decree against women." She was as close to Francis as his own body and soul. Without having received his message, she had known to bring everything he wanted for his burial, "the ashen-colored cloth with which to cover his dying body, also many candles, the cloth for his head, a certain sweetmeat the saint had wanted to eat, and everything the spirit of this man had wanted."[94]

Francis needed to see in Lady Jacoba the affirmation of his physicality that he himself could not provide. By providing for his body, even a sweetmeat (marzipan, according to some sources) for this extreme ascetic, she completed for him his lifelong task of bringing his feminine nature to consciousness. He did not need Clare when he was dying because he had actualized the feminine spirituality in his nature that he had previously projected onto her, but he needed Lady Jacoba for the side of him that he could only see and accept in her face. As Sharp notes, "No matter where a man is in terms of psychological development, he is always prone to see aspects of his anima, his soul, in an actual woman."[95]

The extraordinary place Lady Jacoba held in the life of Francis, a place confirmed by the reverent tone of the normally misogynistic Celano when he speaks of her, is underscored in the event that took place after Francis died: "She was led quietly, streaming with tears, to Francis and his body was placed in her arms....She wept hot tears over his body, wept aloud, and sighed deeply; and holding him in her arms and kissing him, she loosened the veil so that she could see him unhindered."[96] Celano goes on to say that she then saw the stigmata, which had been hidden from all but Francis's closest companions, and recommended that "it should be unveiled before the eyes of all."[97]

This closest of Francis's companions is suppressed in Bonaventure's *The Life of Saint Francis,* the biography that supplanted Celano's versions later in the century, and in Giotto's frescoes in the basilica in Assisi that are based on Bonaventure's version. Bonaventure only mentions Lady Jacoba in the context of a series of miraculous animal stories, recounting that Francis once gave her a lamb that accompanied her to church. Giotto does not depict her at all. However Celano, writing closer to the time of Francis's death and on the basis of eyewitness accounts, includes this extraordinarily intimate encounter between Francis and the embodiment of his anima in his book on miracles. Although Celano's understanding of the miracle is in Lady Jacoba's arrival with everything Francis needed, it was perhaps equally miraculous that the dying ascetic could allow Lady Jacoba to affirm his physicality. Lady Jacoba's unique place in Francis's life was acknowledged by others than Celano. Her funeral urn, though obscurely marked, is on the shelf at the top of the stairs that lead to Francis's tomb in the basilica in Assisi.

Lady Jacoba, Clare, and his mother, Lady Pica, were the outer figures who helped Francis become acquainted with his anima. However, the anima also reveals itself through inner figures. Dreams, fantasy, and prayer can all lead to a relationship with a man's feminine nature. Like the shadow, the anima has two dimensions, one personal and the other archetypal. The personal anima is related to the peculiarities of a man's unique life situation. His understanding of maternal energy comes through his relationship with his mother, and his sexual knowledge comes from a flesh-and-blood lover. But the feminine also has an archetypal dimension buried in the unconscious. While living women can constellate some of this energy, it is too powerful for any one woman to carry. That is why inner figures, religious and mythical personages, and artistic depictions are needed.

In *The Second Life of Saint Francis,* Celano traces a series of inner figures in fantasies and dreams that helped lead Francis along his psycho-spiritual journey. The first occurs in the context of the dream of the palace full of knightly arms. Francis was shown in a vision "a splendid palace in which he saw various military apparatus and a most beautiful bride."[98] Francis misinterpreted this dream: "A carnal spirit prompted him to make a carnal interpretation of the dream, while a far more glorious interpretation lay hidden in the treasures of God's wisdom."[99] Francis's consciousness was still operating at a literal level. He thought he would be a knight and make a good marriage. He needed more encounters with his anima to understand the symbolism of the dream.

Francis's next encounter with his anima was in her dark, frightening manifestation. Francis was by this time consciously trying to relinquish the world. As Celano puts it, "beneath his secular garb he wore a religious spirit."[100] Because the process of individuation is constellated by the energy of opposites, Francis, deep in prayer, was now threatened by the devil who "put into his mind a certain woman who was monstrously hunchbacked, an inhabitant of his city, and who was a hideous sight to all. She threatened to make him like her if he did not leave off what he had begun."[101] Francis, who is tentatively trying to get in touch with his soul, is warned that the quest will transform him into an outcast of society in the deformed body of a woman. At first his anima is his collective doom rather than his individual salvation.

Francis needed to look at this hideous representation of his anima. It was the opposite of the beautiful bride he had been hoping for. Jung understood the process of individuation in terms of opposites: "The repressed content must be made conscious so as to produce a tension of opposites, without which no forward motion is possible....Life is born only of the spark of opposites."[102] The hideous vision of the deformed woman does indeed move Francis along on his journey. It is right after this encounter with the frightening aspect of his anima that he finds the courage to encounter his shadow projected onto the leper. Francis's psycho-spiritual journey will be the opposite of all his former expectations. Until Francis encountered the opposite of his conscious image of the feminine, he was unable to act on his convictions. His religious spirit was worn "beneath his secular garb." It was not actualized. The encounter with his unconscious gave Francis the moral courage to accept the reality of his own unconscious shadow, which he had projected onto the outcasts of Assisi. He could now kiss the leper and shed his former persona because he had overcome his fear of the devil's threat.

After Francis had encountered the opposite extremes of his anima in the personification of the bride and the hunchback, he was able to imagine her in terms of a transformed chivalry. Jung calls this the *Helen stage* of anima development in a man. Francis gave this stage a unique twist. For most men, the *Helen stage* is the transition from idealizing the personal mother and other women to projecting the feminine ideal onto a collective sexual icon—in Jung's terminology, Helen of Troy. In our culture, movie stars and singers often carry the Helen stage of projection. In Francis's age of chivalry, this energy was projected onto an unattainable noblewoman. Although this ideal woman could never be possessed, the meaning of life was in the attempt to be worthy of her. Francis shifted this collective ideal, expressed in the songs of the troubadours, onto Lady

Poverty. Her paradoxical title encompassed the law of opposites that he had learned from his encounter with the vision of the hunchback. The nobility that he aspired to and the poverty that he feared were now united in his marriage with Lady Poverty. Unlike a secular knight, Francis could marry his lady. His life mission became defending his bride from all who would defile her.

Francis's shift from the collective ideal of the unattainable lady of chivalry to the inner figure of Lady Poverty was a milestone on his individuation journey. He was beginning to think symbolically. According to Jung, a symbol is the best possible representation of something in the unconscious. It resonates with meaning beyond, or below, conscious articulation. Lady Poverty was such a symbol for Francis. He accepted her without reservation as the embodiment of his feminine ideal.

The image of a sacred marriage as the bringing together of opposites is a powerful symbol in Carl Jung's investigations of religions and cultures throughout the world. Its prevalence as a symbol suggests its power as an embodiment of archetypal energy. That Francis's unconscious provided him with Lady Poverty as his bride suggests the depth of his connection with his anima. The collective culture's icon of the unattainable lady was inadequate to his deepest yearning. The ideal lady embodied perfection, something unattainable on earth. However, Lady Poverty, as the embodiment of contradictions, was a goal attainable in the process of trying to attain her. She was, in the language of cultural cliché, Francis's better half, who would guide him for the rest of his life. Thousands of men died trying to rescue Helen of Troy. Understood metaphorically, they died because they were fighting for a collective ideal rather than for their own woman. A man must discover his own image of Woman, to whom he can be uniquely wed, if he is to move out of the collective realm and discover his own soul.

All this talk of Lady Poverty and sacred marriage sounds far removed from life, but it was not at all so for Francis. He took his marriage vows very literally and fought to protect the honor of his bride. Francis's devotion to his lady was so complete and literal that he once tried to destroy by hand a chapter house (the room where monks meet for discussion and instruction) that had been built in his absence for a meeting of the friars at the Portiuncola below Assisi. With the spontaneity and emotionalism of the anima, Francis "got up on the roof and with strong hands tore off the slates and tiles. He also commanded the brothers to come up and to tear down completely this monstrous thing contrary to poverty."[103] It took a knight to stop him by explaining that the building belonged to Assisi and not to the friars.

Lady Poverty inflamed Francis's heart with zeal and inspired him to action, but she was not his only inner anima figure. Francis also had a profound relationship with the Virgin Mary. Lady Poverty and the Virgin both belonged to what Jung called the *Mary stage* in a man's anima development. This is the stage when he develops religious feelings. Francis was fortunate to live in an age when the Virgin was a living symbol for the entire culture. Most people today cannot see beyond the image of the Virgin to her symbolic resonance as vehicle of Christ's incarnation and mediator of spirit and matter.[104]

Jung understood the Virgin as a critical symbol to complete the Christian Godhead. He believed that the Christian concept of the Trinity was incomplete as a symbolic representation of the archetype of God. He felt that it left out both the feminine and the dark side of the wholeness that is God. The triune God was Father begetting Son begetting the Holy Spirit. Neither evil nor the feminine were included. According to Jung, because God's opposites were omitted from the collective understanding of divinity, they were relegated to, and unregulated in, the unconscious, coming to consciousness through misogynist projections onto women and through the devil as the carrier of evil. For Jung, the Virgin was a foil to this repression. Jung was jubilant when the Catholic Church made her assumption into heaven a dogma because he believed her presence in heaven would help heal the Godhead, and thus the collective unconscious, by making it more complete.

Francis's devotion to the Virgin suggests that he too, though through mystical experience rather than Jung's scientific observation of myths and art, experienced *quaternity* as a symbol of God's archetypal wholeness. In his *Salutation of the Blessed Virgin,* after greeting her with the courtesy of the chivalric age, Francis includes the Virgin with the other members of the Trinity:

> Hail, O Lady,
> holy Queen,
> Mary, holy Mother of God:
> you are the virgin made church
> and the one chosen by the most holy Father in heaven
> whom he consecrated
> with his most holy beloved Son
> and with the Holy Spirit, the Paraclete,
> in Whom there was and is
> all the fullness of grace and every good.[105]

The quaternity generated when the Virgin is included with Father, Son, and Holy Spirit is an archetypal image of wholeness found in all cultures and religions as well as in dreams and art. Its most potent symbolic representation in Christianity is the cross. Jung perceived the cross as the image made by the four points of quaternity.[106] He found it to be a universal image of wholeness that "has in addition the highest possible moral and religious significance for Western man."[107] Francis had a special reverence for the cross, treating even crossed sticks with respect. Celano asks, "Who can express, who can understand how far Francis was from glorying in anything *save in the cross of our Lord.*"[108] Francis's devotion to the cross, a symbol of quaternity, was nurtured by his affinity to, and compassion for, the humanity of Christ, especially Christ suffering on the cross, rather than by Jung's intellectual understanding of the significance of the number four.

Some medieval mystics perceived Christ's suffering through the symbolic imagery of maternal love. They saw Christ as a nursing mother with his wounds providing the nourishing blood of salvation. Clare had a mystical vision of this nature, but in her dream it was Francis, not Christ, who appeared to her. Peterson describes this dream in which Clare constellates Francis's feminine, nurturing anima. Clare is climbing a long flight of stairs carrying a bowl of hot water and a towel. She is bringing Francis purification in the feminine aspect of a bowl and water. In turn, he offers her his breast, and quoting Christ, he says, "Come, take, and drink."[109] After she drinks from both breasts, the nipple remains in her mouth. When she removes it, it is like a golden mirror. This dream suggests that Francis, through the feminine image of lactation, is able to give Clare what is most precious, the gold that can mirror the mystic's goal. By assisting each other and working through feminine energy, they can transform matter, and each other, into a mirror of God.

Because the Gothic period of the twelfth and thirteenth centuries saw the feminine assume more importance in the collective understanding of the divine, both through the cult of the Virgin and through mystical experience of

Christ's feminine nature, Christ in his humanity, rather than in his divinity, became a common theme. Iconography reflected this shift by transforming the virile, triumphant Christ into a less powerful, more feminine image of the suffering or dead Christ. As Christ's humanity became consciously realized, his humble birth from a woman was introduced as a subject for mystical contemplation.

Francis used Christ's birth as a focal point for a new form of mystical experience. While Neoplatonic mysticism was ahistorical and transcendent, Francis's mysticism was rooted in an historical event. It was powered by anima energy, characterized earlier in this chapter as "the life of the flesh, the life of concreteness, of earth, of emotionality, directed toward people and things." It was very concrete and human.

Francis inaugurated this new form of mysticism in a public way at Grecchio in 1223 by creating a living crèche. The event is commemorated by Giotto in the basilica in Assisi. Bonaventure's inscription reads: "In memory of the birth of Christ at Bethlehem, Francis wanted to reproduce the scene. He asked that a crib be prepared, straw fetched, and an ox and ass be brought to the crib. He then gave a sermon about the birth of the poor King. While he was in prayer, a knight present for this ceremony saw the Infant Jesus come and take the place of the baby Francis had placed in the crib."[110] In Giotto's fresco, Francis, surrounded by his friars and the townspeople of Grecchio, is tenderly placing the Christ child in the manger. Neither Mary nor Joseph is present in the scene. It is as if Francis, through mystical participation, has given birth to the Christ child in thirteenth-century Grecchio.

Ewert Cousins calls Francis's new mystical awareness "mysticism of the historical event." In this type of consciousness, one recalls a significant event from the past, enters into its drama, and draws from it spiritual energy, eventually moving beyond the event toward union with God.[111] This form of mysticism came to dominate Western contemplation. It is also similar to a technique Jung discovered for communicating with the unconscious. Jung called his technique "active imagination."

Jung explains that in active imagination, "You choose a dream, or some other fantasy-image, and concentrate on it by simply catching hold of it and looking at it."[112] Whereas the mystic fixes on an historical event of religious significance, the psychologically oriented person concentrates on an inner event or figure: "You then fix this image in the mind and concentrate on it. Usually it will alter, as the mere fact of contemplating it animates it."[113] The act of contemplation activates energy, just as energy is released by the mystic's participation. The mystic moves toward union with God. The active imaginer is "an acting and suffering figure in the drama of the psyche...as if the drama being enacted before your eyes were real."[114] Just as the goal of historical mysticism is union with God, the goal of active imagination is "to integrate the statements of the unconscious, to assimilate their compensatory content, and thereby produce a whole meaning which alone makes life worth living, and, for not a few people, possible at all."[115] The psycho-spiritual goals are essentially the same in active imagination and mysticism of the historical event. Both are an experience of meaning that is informed by, but finally transcends, the initial stimuli.

Francis's devotion to the humanity of Christ, which inspired him to inaugurate devotion to the nativity, derived from his feminine energy. His capacity to intuit his way into the meaning of an historical event, and through it to God, suggests that his anima was his ally in enabling him to communicate with his unconscious "God within."

Francis's anima energy also enabled him to experience connectedness and transcendence through the natural world. Cousins explains the distinction between this aspect of Francis's mysticism and the thrust of Neoplatonism: "As is the case with the mysticism of the historical event, this is a far cry from Neoplatonic speculative mysticism, which focuses quickly on cosmological structure and which turns quickly from the material world and its individual creatures to scale the metaphysical ladder to the spiritual and divine realms by means of universal concepts."[116]

Francis's mystical awareness found God immanent in the natural world rather than using the natural world as the first rung on the ladder of abstraction to the world of ideal forms. Celano describes Francis's visceral experience of God's immanence:

> Who would be able to narrate the sweetness he enjoyed while contemplating in creatures the wisdom of their Creator, his power and his goodness? Indeed, he was very often filled with a wonderful and ineffable joy from this consideration while he looked upon the sun, while he beheld the stars and the firmament....Toward little worms even he glowed with a very great love.[117]

Francis's concrete anima energy enabled him to see the Creator in every aspect of creation. His anima enabled him to express his vision of unity in the Canticle of Brother Sun that he wrote at the end of his life. The Canticle, which will be explored in a later chapter, reflects the fourth stage of anima consciousness which Jung called the *Sophia* stage, from the biblical name for wisdom. Sophia is a man's guide into his unconscious. She leads him to the source of all symbols and enables him to express what he discovers on the inner journey.

In his *Salutation of the Virtues,* Francis personified Wisdom as the queen of her sister virtues. Using chivalric/religious language, he expressed Jung's later psychological insight that the ego must let go of its assumptions if the anima is to become a living symbol:

> There is surely no one in the entire world
> who can possess any one of you
> unless he dies first.[118]

Jung understood a man's anima as the opposite of his persona. As long as a man's ego tenaciously clings to his persona, his anima will remain unconscious. But if a man comes to know the archetypal anima through the mechanism of projection, she will finally lead him to his own soul. In the religious paradigm of Christianity, Wisdom leads a man to consciousness of the indwelling of the Holy Spirit. When he finally recognizes his own soul, he sees that it is the indwelling of God, one in essence with the Holy Spirit that, through Christ's incarnation, moves through all creation. Jung and Francis are united in their humility before the revelation of the essence of the human soul. In words that could easily come from the mouth of Francis, Jung insists, "We are no more than the stable in which the Lord is born."[119]

In his *Salutation*, Francis pairs the virtues as sisters. Simplicity is the sister of Wisdom. She destroys "all the wisdom of this world/and the wisdom of the body."[120] Simplicity's sister is Holy Wisdom, which "destroys Satan and all his subtlety."[121] Holy Wisdom is the Virgin trampling the serpent under her heel. Evil is vanquished by spiritualized feminine energy.[122]

Although the wisdom of this world is destroyed during the psycho-spiritual journey, the goodness of creation, unblemished by the ego's distortions, remains. Whereas the wisdom of the world creates multiplicity and division,

Holy Simplicity discovers its underlying unity. Francis felt connected to the earth and the elements, to wolves and birds and worms, to Sultan Al-Kamil and Pope Innocent III, to the powerful Cardinal Hugolino and to the simplest of his friars. Because of his sense of connection, he wanted the harmony he experienced within to be mirrored in the outer world. It was his interior peace that enabled him to project peace onto the world.

Jung too understood the need for inner work to transform the outer world. When asked if the world could be saved from cataclysmic destruction, he responded that it could if enough people did their inner work.

Francis was able to bring moments of harmony to the turbulent thirteenth century because of his inner work. He was, in the words of his own prayer, "inwardly cleansed, interiorly enlightened, and inflamed by the fire of the Holy Spirit."[123] He was in touch with his own soul. Because of his intimate relationship with his anima or soul, Francis could be empathetic rather than judgmental, spontaneous rather than self-conscious, and warmly emotional rather than coldly rational. Francis's feminine energy flowed through his relationships with others, especially his friars whom he called "lesser brothers" to recollect their humility. Although they were called brothers, Francis sometimes conceived of their relationship in feminine categories. His directive called *Religious Life in Hermitages* illustrates the feminine energy among them: "No more than three or at most four friars should go together to a hermitage to lead a religious life there. Two of these should act as mothers, with the other two, or the other one, as their children. The mothers are to lead the life of Martha [the active life]; the other two the life of Mary Magdalen [the contemplative life]."[124] The relationship among the friars is that of a mother to her children, and the models are women. The friars are to model their sanctity on women as the best exemplars of the balance between an active and a contemplative life. Francis behaved this way himself. In a letter to Brother Leo written in his own hand he says, "I speak to you, my son, as a mother."[125]

Francis's anima energy enabled him to empathize rather than judge others. Once, in the early days of his brother-hood, a new young friar lamented in the middle of the night that he was starving to death from the austerities of their life. Rather than chastising him for his spiritual weak-ness, Francis set out some food and encouraged all the brothers to share a meal because he "did not want the brother to blush from eating alone."[126] Rather than stand-ing apart and judging, he empathized and helped. It was also his anima that let him know when it was time to hand over leadership of his order to others with more adminis-trative ability. Francis dreamed of a hen whose wings could no longer enfold all its chicks. Identifying with that hen and the limitations of maternal love to protect, he enlisted the more masculine energy of Cardinal Hugolino to guide the order through its period of expansion and change.

Besides nurturing relationships, a man's anima can keep him open to new possibilities. In Jung's words, a good rela-tionship with the anima transforms her into "a psychologi-cal function of an intuitive nature, akin to what the primitives mean when they say...'A little bird told me.'"[127] Jung defines intuition as the psychic function that "revels in the garden of magical possibilities as if they were real."[128] It was this intuitive genius, directed by anima energy, that enabled Francis to move with such confidence and creativ-ity. For Francis possibilities were real. He could imagine convincing Innocent III to allow his twelve friars to create a whole new kind of religious order of itinerant men preach-ing poverty and penance to the new urban populations. Innocent, who was at that time refusing to allow any new orders in the church, accepted his plan. Francis understood the need of lay people to live out their spirituality in the world and founded a Third Order for this purpose. He dreamed that an army of his friars spread out over the world. In 1217, over five thousand friars gathered below Assisi for a general chapter meeting of the order before dispersing to missions across the Alps and the Mediterranean. He wanted to be a knight crusading for Christ's peace and managed to become friends with the sultan, the heathen enemy of Christianity.[129]

The next chapter will examine intuition, the wisdom that comes from a man's anima or soul, in the context of the different ways we orient our consciousness on the psycho-spiritual journey.

CHAPTER SIX
Removing the Blinders

The psycho-spiritual process of the individuation journey may be looked at as the gradual removal of blinders. Imagine a horse whose vision is constricted, both to protect him from frightening sights and to keep him going in a straight line. Our psychological orientation functions like a horse's blinders as we develop a conscious personality and a place in the world. It protects us from too many distractions and from sudden scares. Our consciousness, like the horse's vision, is held to the route that leads to the ego's destination. Later, as we become more seasoned travelers and more accustomed to the unexpected sights and sounds along the inner and outer journey, the range of our vision can be expanded. Although we always need the blinders to protect us from more than our consciousness can bear, one of our individuation tasks is to gain some conscious control over the blinders so that we can help adjust their position and gain a wider vision of life's realities and possibilities.

Like the rest of us, Francis started out wearing the blinders of time, class, gender, and family. In previous chapters we have looked at the collective values of the thirteenth century that circumscribed Francis's vision. We saw how he removed the blinders of prejudice against lepers and the myopic cynicism that encouraged people to accept the church as a profoundly flawed and corrupt institution. We

watched him peer around the ramifications of being a merchant's son and reject material gain for the pearl beyond
price. We saw him strip off the persona of his former life
and confront the shadow side of his culture and his own
personality. We also followed him as he became conscious
of his feminine energy, first through projection and then by
moving inward to discover his own soul. In this chapter, by
considering Francis's basic psychological orientation and
how it developed during his psycho-spiritual journey, we
will examine another kind of blinders that both focus and
limit consciousness. But first we will take a quick look at
some of the psychological language and concepts that will
help us consider Francis's journey from Jung's psychological vantage point.

Jung used typology to describe the different ways we perceive and react to the world we wake up to each morning.
He divides people broadly into two types—extraverts and
introverts. Extraverts are energized by people, things, and
ideas in the outer world. They need to plug into something
outside of themselves and are uncomfortable with the flow
of their own psychic energy. Introverts are jolted by too
much external energy. They run on the psychic energy of
their inner nature. Naturally wary of the external world,
they find their own psychic reality more compelling than
people and external events.[130]

Jung's research and experience led him to believe that
our fundamental orientation to the world is a matter of
nature more than nurture. He believed this because children in the same family, raised under essentially identical
circumstances, can differ dramatically in their degree of
introversion or extraversion. We all know families where
this is true. For one child, an experience is not real until it
has been talked about and shared and processed through
other people. Another child in the same family daydreams

and keeps a diary or talks to imaginary friends for his or her authentic life, and only shares what family and school require. As an adult, the extraverted child will need to discover a sacred space within that is impervious to the opinions of others. The introvert will need to learn to empathize with others and accept their empathy, or that sacred space will become an arid desert.

Our culture encourages extraversion. Babies experience day care, where they have to learn to adjust to collective, institutional requirements, before they have begun to develop any ego strength. Then they enter public education, based on the model of a factory, where they must conform to a rigid schedule and constantly interact with adults and children according to collectively acceptable norms of behavior and intellectual output. During their time outside of school, they either engage in structured activities or absorb the messages and images of mass media through such culturally acceptable solitary activities as television, computers, and electronic games. When children play with their friends, their activities and conversation are informed by the images and values that they absorb from television and movies. Children with a high degree of introversion are considered strange. They suffer in schools that are increasingly driven by a model of cooperative learning and communal space. Their need to process the world in a solitary way finds no recognition. They have to develop an unnatural degree of extraversion just to survive.

Francis too grew up in an extraverted culture. Life in Italian cities was very public, centering on communal squares. Family life was public too—houses were close together, and there was no such thing as privacy. Everyone knew everyone else's business. While people in rural Umbria could engage in solitary agricultural work more compatible with an introverted temperament, a naturally introverted urban resident either developed extraversion or was considered very strange.[131]

Francis's Italy was the most urbanized area in Europe. It led the transition from feudal to capitalistic values. So it was in Italy that the clash between extraverted and introverted cultural orientation first became most pronounced in the realm of collective values. Part of Francis's genius was to intuit this tension and to create, through his own life, an example of how to honor both extraversion and introversion. By moving between periods of seclusion and periods of active ministry in the secular world, he demonstrated a rhythm to life that honored both introversion and extraversion.

A few minutes in a bookstore in our own time shows the need we feel for this same kind of balance. Amidst our frantic lifestyle and mass-produced culture, titles encouraging and instructing meditation and the cultivation of an inner life abound. Most of us have to behave like extraverts during the majority of our waking hours, but many of us feel depleted by the experience of adapting to extraverted cultural expectations.

In his first biography, Celano describes the young Francis as an extravert. He was highly sociable and lived according to accepted collective values rather than his own unique way of looking at things. That changed after his conversion experience and his repudiation of his father. Collective values no longer mattered as much as the dictates of the voice of God that he heard within. Yet as he became more introverted, Francis grew in humility rather than in the shyness of a born introvert. He was therefore able to use the richness of his newly discovered inner life to energize his relationships in the outer world. A charismatic figure, Francis used his extraversion to help ground the highly charged current of his inner life. The institutional church, with its symbols, sacraments, and hierarchy of authority, helped to define and contain his encounter with the *Self.*

It is important to think about the need for both introversion and extraversion in the individuation journey. In order to break from collective values and discover one's inner truth, it is necessary to develop a degree of introversion. Yet to be able to return the inner gifts to the outer world, one must be extraverted enough to care about the outer world and be able to function in it. Francis was profoundly tempted by the inner world he discovered to become a hermetic mystic. But his extraversion made him turn to his friends for guidance. Celano reports that Clare advised him to continue his mission in the world. Francis relied on Clare, as the embodiment of his own soul, to direct him in this enormous decision. He spent his life developing a balance between action and contemplation. Celano describes the balance in Francis's life in this way: "It was his custom to divide up the time given him to merit grace, and, as seemed necessary to him, to give part of it to working for the good of his neighbors and the rest to the blessed retirement of contemplation."[132] This balance between extraversion and introversion is one of the most compelling results of his individuation journey.

Francis was willing to forgo the selfish ecstasy of mystical union to honor his extraverted impulse to relate to the outer world. Many wisdom traditions discount mystical union as the apex of spiritual development. They stress the need to bring the treasure of this experience back to the world in the spirit of Buddha or Jesus or Mohammed. One mark of Francis's individuation journey was his willingness to share what he discovered. He introduced to Western consciousness a model for moving between action and contemplation on the Christian spiritual journey, a balance sorely needed in our extraverted age.

Although extraversion or introversion are fundamental to our psychological orientation, typology has another level of differentiation: what Jung calls the four *functions*. The functions describe how we perceive and how we judge our perceptions. Jung calls perceiving irrational, because it is immediate, and judging rational, because it involves evaluation.

According to Jung, there are two ways to perceive the world. At one extreme we experience life primarily through our senses. What is real and meaningful is what we can see or hear or feel or taste or smell. Anything else seems somewhat fanciful. Jung calls this function *sensation*. The other way of perceiving is psychic rather than physical. Possibilities and probabilities have a palpable presence through this function, which Jung calls *intuition*. Intuitives perceive the world in terms of relationships and possibilities unbounded by practical limitations. They find sensing types unimaginative and limited; sensing types find intuitives impractical and irrelevant to solving the immediate challenges of daily life.

After we perceive the world through sensation or intuition—and Jung contends that we generally rely on one at the expense of the other—we have to decide what to do with our perceptions. There are two different systems we can use. We can evaluate the data objectively according to how it fits within a system of logical meaning, or we can consider the data subjectively based on what we value. A *thinking* type is conscious of logic; a *feeling* type is conscious of worth. Jung contends that it is almost impossible to be conscious of both at the same time.

Jung's theory of psychological orientation is modeled on quaternity and the tension of opposites. It is based on his model of archetypal wholeness symbolized by the cross. Our crucifixion is to suffer the consciousness that develops as all four functions are accepted as part of reality. Our ego wants to limit our consciousness in the interests of focus and adaptation. So our ego must suffer as our consciousness expands.

At the beginning of our journey, at least one of the four functions is repressed. We cannot consciously use it. That inferior function contains the missing part of the whole, holy person we are meant to become. The opposite of our greatest strength is our inferior function. For example, if our greatest strength is thinking, then our greatest weakness is feeling. Our logic is paid for by our emotional obtuseness. Or if our greatest strength is intuition, our greatest weakness is sensation. Our imagination comes at the expense of our practicality. Because we have repressed our inferior function in the process of developing a persona and adapting to the external world, using it seems unfamiliar and uncomfortable. However, if we are to become whole persons, we must learn to stretch and grow by becoming conscious of the blinders imposed by our inferior functions.

Although no one is confined exclusively to one way of perceiving and one way of judging, we all tend to limit our perceptions and judgments so that we can focus our consciousness and arrive at decisions. A sensing type tends to overlook the world of possibilities available to the intuitive, whereas the intuitive is apt to be impractical. The thinking type overlooks values, whereas the feeling type can behave quite irrationally on the basis of value judgments that appear irrelevant to the thinking type. One of the individuation tasks is to remove the blinders of our psychological orientations and bring our inferior functions to consciousness. If intuition is our strength, we need to consciously experience life through our senses. If our reliance on sensation keeps us unaware of the potential for change, we need intuition to see the possibilities inherent in our situation. If our decisions are based exclusively on feeling, we need to learn to consider logic. If our decisions are based exclusively on logic, we need to get in touch with our values.

All this brings us, finally, back to Francis, whose life is a study in one man's struggle to balance the introversion of a contemplative life with the extraversion of action in the world. His story also shows how, like the other individuation tasks we have examined so far—bringing the persona, the shadow, and the anima to consciousness—the struggle to become more flexible about perceiving and judging the world both demands and creates consciousness or, in religious language, the enlightenment of the Holy Spirit.

Before his conversion, Francis accepted the external world as the arbiter of perceptions and judgments. He fit in. Nothing stood between him and his experiences; and when he judged what was happening, he used the prevailing logic of his world. If Assisi was at war with Perugia, he fought. If chivalry was what was happening, he aspired to be a knight. His subjective feelings and intuition were less consciously available to him than his physical sensations and the logic of the situation.

For a sensing type, intuition is the most repressed and least developed of the four functions. It is the inferior function that, being the most repressed, has the most potential for conscious growth. Francis's conversion enabled him to access his intuition. Through intuition, he came to realize the enormous potential for change in his world. In his *Testament*, Francis tells us that it was his encounter with a leper that transformed him. His account of that experience describes the coming to consciousness of both intuition and feeling:

> This is how God inspired me, Brother Francis, to embark upon a life of penance. When I was in sin, the sight of lepers nauseated me beyond measure; but then God himself led me into their company and I had pity on them. When I had

once become acquainted with them, what had previously nauseated me became a source of spiritual and physical consolation for me. After that I did not wait long before leaving the world.[133]

In psychological language, God is the archetype of wholeness that impels the development of the total personality. Jung's psychology, like Christianity, is teleological. Life has a purposeful goal that unfolds through time. Individuation is the paradoxical incarnation of the eternal in time. The timeless world of the unconscious manifests through each unique ego, and each finite life becomes immortal through acceptance of the unconscious. This individuation process is never completed in a given lifetime. Francis had to "embark on a life of penance." Another word for penance is *metanoia,* which is a daily conversion to inner truth and outer action. With each new acceptance of consciousness, the ego is strengthened for more, but each stage also involves suffering. Life is a series of crucifixions to allow a fuller realization of the opposites that both comprise and create the whole.

Psychologically, being "in sin" is being caught up in egocentricity at the expense of consciousness. The ego's pride makes it assume a defensive posture against any perceptions or judgments that force it to change. When Francis was in sin, he only perceived lepers through his senses. On the level of sensation, they were disgusting to him. He judged his perceptions with his mind rather than his heart. Since lepers were society's outcasts and physically disgusting, he rejected them.

Francis's growth in consciousness is signaled by his different reaction to lepers after "God himself led me into their company." Seeing the lepers with his inner eye rather than with the collective eye of his culture, Francis "had pity on them." His values became conscious, and he judged lepers with feeling instead of logic. When Francis became more conscious, he was able to say, "What had previously nauseated me became a source of spiritual and physical consolation." The consolation he experienced was the coming to consciousness of intuition and feeling. He now perceived the lepers as his path to salvation. He could use intuition rather than sensation to experience the world. The world he left after that experience was the world of the senses where death is triumphant. His intuition and feeling showed him another world beyond decay.

After his conversion, Francis's use of sensation became introverted. According to Jung, introverted sensation filters the experience of physical reality through subjective consciousness. Francis's conversion experience demonstrates that his sensation became introverted. Because he was plugged into the circuit of his own psyche rather than into the external world, he experienced and judged the external world in a radically different way. A famous event in the Francis legend illustrates this phenomenon. While Francis was praying in the tiny church called San Damiano, the image of Christ painted on the cross spoke to him, saying, "Rebuild my church." Francis's subjective consciousness transformed the objective reality of the painted cross into the subjective experience of Christ speaking to him.[134]

Introverted sensation can be frightening because it erases the distance between subject and object. The object loses its objectivity because the perceiver transforms it according to his own subjective understanding of reality. Introverted sensation can make the external world a place of magical forces that can easily gain control of the ego and annihilate it. It must be mediated by some sort of judgment. Francis dealt with the power of the crucifix by developing a conscious relationship with the values it evoked. He judged it with feeling and used it to constellate a tremendous empathy for Christ.

Francis's introverted experience with the cross at San Damiano was an important marker in his individuation journey. Before his conversion, Francis judged his perception of the crucifix with thinking rather than feeling. His judgment was in keeping with the collective judgment of the church. The church was out of touch with the feeling dimension of religious experience. Instead, it was concerned with building an institution based on rules and dogma and a rigidly controlled flow of experience through images and sacraments. The prevailing image of the crucifix discouraged interaction. Christ was depicted without any evidence of physical anguish. Often he appeared triumphant, even while on the cross. When Francis's intuition and feeling became conscious to him, he began to interact with the image of the crucified Christ. It became a living symbol for him. The crucifix told him, "Rebuild my church." Part of this rebuilding process was to reintroduce feeling and intuition to Christian consciousness. Iconography provides a visual record of this process. Artists began to depict Christ in his agony, sometimes with Francis tenderly embracing his wounded feet.

When sensation turned inward, Francis built on his natural affinity for drama to express his sensations. Whereas previously he had acted in plays in Assisi or decked himself flamboyantly as the rich merchant's son, after his conversion, he dramatized his inner perceptions through the life of a mendicant mystic. He exchanged his lavish clothes for a coarse tunic and reenacted an apostolic life in the thirteenth century.

We will never know exactly what triggered Francis's conversion. We can hypothesize that his imprisonment and illness turned him inward. It is possible that the horrors he observed at the Battle of Collestrada and in prison, as well as his own lengthy illness, caused him to judge his sensations by his own light rather than through the light of his society's values. His depression may have been partially caused by his repressed intuition and feeling. Jung observes that "[a] reversal of type often proves exceedingly harmful to the physiological well-being of the organism, usually causing acute exhaustion."[135] At any rate, the outcome was that Francis's consciousness was ready to receive and judge the image of Christ at San Damiano in a unique and compelling way.

For Francis, the first experience of identification with the suffering Christ was triggered by an object that did not, of itself, suggest a need for empathy. The Christ painted on the cross at San Damiano portrays no suffering. Francis's consciousness supplied Christ's subjective agony. It was his introverted sensation and feeling that transformed the object. Furthermore, because his experience occurred when there was a need for introversion and empathy in the collective realm, his subjective experience of Christ developed into the collective norm for Christian iconography and piety. The influence that Francis's subjective experience exerted suggests that it helped to provide needed direction for the collective values of his age. The church had become both the dispenser of extraverted ritual divorced from subjective resonance and a cynical arena for secular power. Francis's subjective experience of the reality of Christ's suffering brought visceral reality into Christianity. It was one way he heeded the crucifix's call to rebuild the church.[136]

The church Francis was called upon to rebuild provided an institutional container for introverted sensation. Medieval psychology lent a subjective cast to objective reality. The whole phenomenon of the Crusades was triggered by the desecration of holy relics in Jerusalem. Relics are the

Crucifix by the Italian School, 13th century (S. Chiara, Assisi, Italy).

products of introverted sensation. They are objects associated with Christ and Christian saints that are endowed, from their close association with a holy person, with miraculous properties. Because relics fall within a collective framework of beliefs, their miraculous (or, in secular language, magical) attributes are comforting rather than frightening. They behave benignly for the benefit of believers who come within their physical presence. They help sanctify an altar (to this day every altar in a Catholic church must contain a relic), effect cures, and help focus spiritual energy for the benefit of the devout. Medieval Christians underwent incredibly perilous journeys to come within the presence of relics in Jerusalem and other holy places.[137]

Introverted sensation is also the psychology that underlies a sacramental outlook. Sacraments are physical manifestations of the divine intervention in human affairs. The thirteenth century codified the church's sacraments. Most dramatically, the sacrament of the Eucharist was declared to be, quite literally, the body and blood of Christ. What appears through the senses to be bread and wine, introverted sensation knows to be the body and blood of the Savior. Psychic reality prevails over physical evidence.[138]

Introverted sensation can be judged with the mind or with the heart. The church dealt with its sacramental perception of reality by codifying it and regulating its accessibility to the laity. Francis reacted to the sacraments, particularly the Eucharist, with his heart. He was not moved by the logical edifice on which its reality was elaborately constructed, although he accepted all the pronouncements of the Fourth Lateran Council. What moved him was the reality of Christ's physical presence in the world. In his *Testament* he said, "In this world I cannot see the most high Son of God with my own eyes, except for his most holy body and blood which they [priests] receive and they alone administer to others."[139] Francis respected all priests, no matter how corrupt, because of their power to renew the Incarnation through the sacrament of the Eucharist. His introverted sensation was bounded by the container of the church's hierarchical prescriptions.

Although Francis's thinking function accepted the logical edifice of Catholic theology, his more consciously available feeling function, coupled with introverted sensation, enabled him to bring events in the life of Christ emotionally alive for himself and his followers (discussed in the previous chapter as mysticism of the historical event). The two most dramatic examples of this mystical experience in Francis's life occurred at Grecchio and LaVerna. At Grecchio he and the other participants entered into the mystery of the Incarnation by perceiving Christ's birth through introverted sensation using physical props of the manger scene. At LaVerna he experienced Christ's crucifixion.

Extraverted intuition is the function that finds the possibilities inherent in a situation. Unlike extraverted *sensation,* which accepts existing conditions as a given, extraverted *intuition* is looking for change. It is a particularly valuable function when sensation, thinking, and feeling have no capacity to show a way out. Francis's capacity to use intuition to get out of a tough situation is shown in his confrontation with his father. The facts of the case were that he had stolen from his father and was, according to collective morality, a bad son. But Francis saw a way to dramatize his situation, taking it beyond the mores of Assisi. By transferring his allegiance from his biological father to his heavenly one and returning all his earthly possessions, he appealed to a higher morality. Jung notes the dramatic intensity of the intuitive as he becomes caught up in his vision of how things *could* be: "He brings his vision to life, he presents it convincingly and with dramatic fire. He embodies it, so to speak. But this is not play acting, it is a kind of fate."[140] Francis had enjoyed acting in plays in Assisi.[141] But he was not play acting in front of the cathedral. As Jung puts it, "The stronger his intuition, the more his ego becomes fused with all the possibilities he envisions."[142] Francis's ego identified with the insight that the pearl of great price demanded of him absolute poverty and required a renunciation of his father's values.

By the standards of this world, it was a heartless act to repudiate his father, and by extension his family, in front of the whole community. But Francis, like Jesus, was responding to the vision of the intuitive who cannot accept the boundaries of conventional relationships. Recall Matthew's account of Jesus:

> While he was still speaking to the crowds, his mother and brothers appeared outside wishing to speak with him. [Someone told him, "Your mother and your brothers are standing outside, asking to speak with you."] But he said in reply to the one who told him, "Who is my mother? Who are my brothers?" And stretching out his hand toward his disciples, he said, "Here are my mother and my brothers. For whoever does the will of my heavenly Father is my brother, and sister, and mother."[143]

Like Jesus' dismissal of his earthly family, Francis's repudiation of his father went against this world's understanding of loyalty and made no practical sense. He was giving up his birthright and acting ridiculous for no ostensible reason. The morality of his decision was tied up with his vision of a radically new life. For Francis, as for Jesus, practicality or consideration of the immediate welfare of himself and others had no part in what he was doing.

Why was Francis able to use his intuition at this critical juncture to dramatize his inner situation to himself and the people of Assisi? Perhaps there is a connection between introverted sensation and intuition. While extraverted sensation stays in the immediacy of sensate reality, introverted sensation, as discussed above, creates a subjective understanding of the object that can, like intuition, move away from the present moment. Francis's perception of the crucifix moved back in time to the historical event and forward in time to a new understanding of the image. Introverted sensation, like intuition, sees new possibilities in the world of perceptions. Thus it seems possible that Francis's conversion experience, which moved his sensation inward, also brought his intuition to the threshold of consciousness, a threshold which was crossed when events became so complex that only intuition could find a way out.

Francis's intuition rescued him again when he was attempting to get his fledgling order recognized by Innocent III. The objective facts of the matter were that he and his bedraggled group of followers had come to Rome to ask the pope, who had decided to control the risk of heresy by putting a cap on any new orders in the church, to approve a radically new conception of religious life—monks who left the cloister to preach in the world. There was no logical reason for Innocent to entertain his proposal. However, Francis had a vision of a new order that could help reform the church. He communicated his vision so powerfully to the skeptical Innocent that the pope had a dream in which Francis was literally holding up the Roman basilica that is the seat of the church. Giotto captures this dream in the basilica in Assisi. In his fresco, the Lateran is leaning toward the sleeping pope ready to crush him. Francis holds it up, preventing it from collapsing.

On the strength of this dream, Innocent gave Francis permission to preach in the world, a right that had been given exclusively to the clergy in the interests of preserving dogmatic purity. Francis's intuitive understanding of the force and rightness of his vision of a new preaching order prevailed.

Extraverted intuition enabled Francis to translate his conversion experience into a vision of a transformed outer world. Using intuition, he perceived the world in terms of possibilities rather than practical realities, and, relying on feeling, he conveyed his vision by the force of personal relationships rather than through a philosophic or institutional system. Because of his highly developed intuition, he saw that his world could be transformed. For a sensing type, intuition is the most repressed and least developed of the four functions. It is the inferior function that, being the most repressed, has the most potential for conscious growth. Francis's conversion enabled him to access his intuition. Through intuition, he came to realize the enormous potential for change in his world. And because of the passion of his convictions and the warmth of his empathy, he could make others share his vision of a renewed world transformed by living apostolic values.

The availability of extraverted intuition to Francis's consciousness had a compensatory side in his unconscious. Because he came to rely on extraverted intuition rather than on extraverted sensation to deal with the outer world, his conscious attitude toward sensations that contradicted his ideal vision was one of disdain. He despised his body with its appetites and needs; he feared women as possible sources of temptation; and he rejected money as intrinsically evil, not even allowing his friars to so much as touch it for any purpose. His conscious attitude about his body and sex and money fits in with his vision of a life of apostolic poverty. But the Francis who once ate, drank, enjoyed women, and spent his father's money did not disappear. He just went underground. The vehemence of Francis's reaction to physicality and money suggests the struggle it cost him to maintain his conscious position of control. When sensation became introverted, all physical objects assumed a subjective cast. His body lost its objective reality and became an impediment to his identification with Christ. Money too became an obstacle to spiritual development and lost any objective usefulness.

Deprived of their immediate reality as objects, money and the human body acquired magical power. Francis judged them harshly because they had no place in his vision of apostolic poverty. Jung describes the negative side effects of extraverted intuition: "His conscious attitude toward both [extraverted] sensation and object is one of ruthless superiority....But sooner or later the object takes revenge in the form of compulsive hypochondriacal ideas, phobias, and every imaginable kind of absurd bodily sensation."[144] Francis suffered various ailments throughout his life. His repression of a desire to eat manifested itself in severe gastrointestinal problems, possibly exacerbated by his habit of mixing ashes into his meager nourishment to make it even more unpalatable. His repressed sexuality made him afraid to even look at a woman and inspired extreme acts of mortification. Celano reports that Francis and his brothers, "tried to repress the promptings of the flesh with such great mortification that often they did not refrain from stripping themselves naked in the coldest weather and from piercing their bodies all over with the points of thorns, even to causing the blood to flow."[145]

Francis's repressed interest in money also made him overreact to its power to corrupt. An anecdote from Celano's second biography illustrates Francis's extreme reaction. When a friar picked up some money a lay person had left at the Portiuncula, Francis "commanded him to lift the money from the window sill with his mouth and to place it with his mouth on the asses' dung outside the walls of the place."[146] These incidents demonstrate that Francis's repressed extraverted sensation sometimes cost him consciousness of a balanced, compassionate approach to the world of objects.

Paradoxically, Francis's attempt to deny his own physicality through extreme asceticism led, finally, to his receiving the stigmata. God would not allow Francis to dismiss the external world as an avenue of grace. He used Francis's own body, the most despised object of all, to imprint the message of his immanence in all creation. Francis tried to reject his body as a source of grace. He accepted the reality of incarnation for Christ but not for himself. His receiving the stigmata forced him to consciously accept the indwelling of God in his own despised body.[147] His individuation journey required that he move from the young Francis who valued his body for the pleasure it gave him to the mature Francis who experienced it as the way to participate in the Incarnation.

Francis's extraverted intuition cost him his extraverted sensation, repurchased through the stigmata. It also contributed to his inability to lead the order he had founded. Jung describes the restlessness of the intuitive, a restlessness that in Francis was manifested in a lifelong series of journeys throughout Italy and in quest for martyrdom at various crusade battlefields. As Jung says, "Always [the intuitive] must be running after a new possibility, quitting his newly planted fields while others garner in the harvest."[148] Francis had the vision, but he could not take practical steps to realize it. He had no talent for administration and no interest in leadership. He insisted that Franciscan spirituality be based on humility and service.

Francis had a vision of thousands of friars bringing the fervor of a renewed Christianity to the farthest corners of the earth, so in 1219 he left Italy for an eighteen-month trip to the East. During this time, others had the opportunity to redirect his order, and their deviation from the original purity of his vision was the greatest sorrow of his life. His departure at this critical juncture is only explicable as a manifestation of his psychological orientation. Francis's powerful intuition of a rebuilt church and his empathy with Christ that energized this intuition, cost him the practicality and logic to stay home and "gather in the harvest." In a sense, he had to trade one set of blinders for another. That necessity is part of our individuation too. To exist in space and time as one unique manifestation of creation is to accept defining limitations. The real question is whose blinders we will choose, those that are externally imposed or those that come from within to guide us on our own unique path.

Francis's blinders caused him acute spiritual suffering when he returned to find his order so changed. The University of Bologna had been established, leading to an intellectualizing of Franciscan spirituality. Many friars were living a settled life in permanent structures. The church was directing the order as an ecclesiastical institution. Francis's intuitive vision of apostolic life was being dimmed by practical necessity. While this was happening, he went blind. It was as if his body resonated with the pain of events in the outer world to such an extent that it physically turned his vision inward. With the dramatic literalness that characterized him, Francis was blinded by his inferior function.

Francis's powerful use of intuition demonstrates how our authentic blinders both focus and limit the scope of our journey. His mission to rebuild the church called for a shift in consciousness toward *feeling*. Francis was in touch, through his feeling function, with powerful emotions. He could lead by the charismatic force of his highly charged personal presence, but he paid for his consciousness of personal and archetypal emotions with an estrangement from creativity in the areas of logic and practical organization.[149] Francis literally did not know how to think for himself. When he returned from the East in 1220, he relinquished control of his order to others with administrative ability and watched in despair as his ideals were modified to fit the demands of a more settled, permanent life.[150]

Looking at Francis's psycho-spiritual journey through the psychological model of typology, two things are striking. First was his evolution from an extraverted young man into a mystic with an intense inner life based on events in the outer world. He was a contemplative man of action or an active contemplative. The second noteworthy characteristic of Francis's psychological orientation was his capacity to consciously access three out of four functions to an almost equal degree. Only the thinking function was inferior, both in his inner and his outer life.

Francis's introverted *sensation* enabled him to identify with Christ through spiritual discipline and emotional empathy. It also enabled him to transform the chivalric ideal of courtly love for some unattainable lady in the real world into dedication to Lady Poverty, an inner figure. He used his sensation in an introverted fashion to create an inner universe of meaning and relationship.

Francis also made extraverted use of his *intuition*. It enabled him to transform his conversion experience into a vision of a transformed outer world. Using intuition, he perceived the world in terms of possibilities rather than practical realities; and relying on *feeling,* he conveyed his vision by the force of personal relationships rather than through a philosophic or institutional system. Because of his highly developed intuition, he saw that his world could be transformed. And because of the passion of his convictions and the warmth of his empathy, he could make others share his vision of a renewed world transformed by living apostolic values.

Francis was like the rest of us in being blinded by his inferior function. He was, however, remarkable in the extent to which he developed and integrated his three other functions and in his capacity to be energized through both extraversion and introversion. It is perhaps this balance of action and contemplation that is the most important model Francis can offer us today. Like Francis, we must both spend time listening to God speak to us from whatever contemporary crucifix he chooses, and have the courage to live out his plan for our life. We need the courage to remove the blinders of our extraverted culture and the wisdom to accept the unique blinders that define our authentic path on the inner journey and back out into the world.

CHAPTER SEVEN
La Verna

In September of 1224, Francis achieved the martyrdom
that eluded him at Damietta. The years after his return
from the East in 1220 had been painful ones. His health
was rapidly deteriorating, and he felt isolated from the
order he had founded. He handed over leadership to Peter
Cataneo, who was rapidly succeeded by Brother Elias, one
of Francis's most intimate brothers and one of the most
enigmatic figures in the history of the Franciscan Order.[151]
Under pressure from the church, he exiled himself to Fonte
Colombo to write a new rule for the order, a painful under-
taking for a man of his typology. In the course of political
wrangling among those in the order who wanted a more
pragmatic, less strenuous rule, Francis's original draft was
"lost." In 1223 he drafted another rule, this one following
the legislative dictates of Cardinal Hugolino rather than
the intuition and feeling of his own heart and soul, which
was adopted at the 1224 Chapter. Francis had become a
mere figurehead of the order. In the process, he had undergone a wrenching martyrdom of both his ego and his
ideals. He was experiencing physical martyrdom too, with a
host of ailments dominated by a painful eye condition that
was costing him his sight. Soon all these forms of suffering,
as well as decades dedicated to intense identification with
Christ's suffering, would come to a dramatic climax.

While at LaVerna, a mountain hermitage in Tuscany given to him by Count Orlando of Chiusi in 1213, Francis had a vision and received the five wounds of Christ in his hands, feet, and right side. This chapter examines Francis's unique experience of martyrdom exploring thirteenth-century written and visual accounts of the event as both literal fact and spiritual allegory. It also treats Francis's vision and stigmata as an archetypal continuation of the religious myth of Christianity in which, through the Incarnation, a transcendent God becomes immanent in creation. Francis thus becomes a symbol for us of our own potential unity with God.

Edward Edinger[152] speaks of individuation as the process of developing the ego-Self axis. The conscious ego becomes aware of the unconscious Self through activities such as prayer, meditation, dreams, and creative work. By letting go of conscious control, the ego can communicate with the unconscious through symbols. The ego can then experience the meaning of the symbols and become more aware of the richness of the unconscious Self. The axis that Edinger speaks of is the conduit or channel that is formed by the ego's willingness to experience messages from the unconscious. In religious language, it is the power of the Holy Spirit. Francis's contemplative experiences, powerful dreams, and openness to synchronicity prepared him for the vision and stigmata at LaVerna.

The first account of Francis's stigmatization is in a letter written by Brother Elias, the minister general of the Franciscan Order at the time of Francis's death. Elias writes enthusiastically to the French provincial minister about "a new miracle," unparalleled since "the case of the Son of God, Who is Christ the Lord."[153] Brother Elias reports that Francis's stigmata signals a new human experience, the miraculous identification of a man with Christ. He states that this event is the most joyful thing to happen to humankind since the Incarnation. Then God participated in human suffering. Now a man has shared the suffering of God incarnate. Elias was the first of many in the thirteenth century to suggest that Francis's miraculous experience paralleled that of Christ and opened up new possibilities for human transformation.

A miracle is "a wonderful event, transcending the known laws of nature, due to supernatural intervention."[154] In the religious paradigm, the "supernatural intervention" comes from divine interaction with the physical world. In the world of miracles, observable laws of cause and effect are provisional. Through the intervention of a saint or a holy relic or prayer, nature's laws can be bent to fit human need. The blind can see, water becomes wine, a lover of Christ receives his wounds.

Supernatural intervention also occurs in Jung's paradigm of the individuation journey. Jung observed acausal relationships between the psyche and physical events that suggest an underlying unity between the physical and spiritual worlds. He called such relationships *synchronicity,* a "meaningful coincidence"[155] in which external events symbolize what is happening in the psyche. Jung posits that matter and the psyche are essentially only different forms of energy. Synchronicity is the "acausal connecting principle"[156] between the unconscious and physical events.

Both synchronicity and miracles imply an underlying unity between the world of sense perceptions and another unseen world, and both offer hope of healing the apparent rift between spirit and matter. Part of the individuation journey is the willingness to look for patterns in times of seeming chaos and to be open to the significance of "coincidences." To appreciate synchronicity, we must be "in sync" with the correspondence between external events and the workings of the unconscious.

Jung cited one example of a synchronistic event in the course of an analysis. His analysand was struggling to understand a dream about the Egyptian beetle, a sacred symbol of birth. As she was recounting her dream, a beetle scratched at the window by Jung's desk. He opened the window and caught the beetle. That event marked the beginning of transformation, or rebirth, for the analysand. The beetle's appearance provided a conduit for the unconscious to communicate a new attitude to her conscious mind.[157]

For Francis, the stigmata was a physical manifestation of his psycho-spiritual identification with Christ. Just as Jung's analysand needed an event in the physical world to enflesh the rebirth potentially available in her unconscious, Francis needed the stigmata to realize his own participation in divinity. Synchronicity is one way that God can alert us to his presence, and, according to Jung, "the saints who received the stigmata became Christ-figures in a visible and concrete way."[158]

Long before the miracle Elias cited, Francis's journey was full of less dramatic examples of synchronicity. Being a sensing type, Francis often had to move through a physical experience to acquire conscious understanding. In contemporary educational jargon, we would call him a kinesthetic learner; that is, he had to experience something through his body before he could understand it with his conscious mind. Remember Francis rebuilding all those churches around Assisi after the cross at San Damiano spoke to him? He had to hear the cross speak to him before he could hear his own inner voice telling him to begin a new journey.[159] Then he had to physically rebuild those churches rock by rock to build an understanding of the church as a complex system of beliefs, rituals, and flawed human beings all in need of repair.

For many of us, our bodies alert us to spiritual needs. Difficulty swallowing; neck, back, and stomach ailments; and a variety of other symptoms, when interpreted symbolically, can signal the need for inner transformation. Like Francis, we sometimes need to work on the transformation from the outside. We may need to alter or leave a job or relationship or find a creative outlet. Or, like Francis, we may need a physical journey to begin our inner journey. Francis walked hundreds of kilometers in the course of his spiritual journey. His monastic cells, often in caves, are spread throughout Umbria and Tuscany. He seemed to need physical movement to precipitate and mirror his spiritual journey. So one of the messages of LaVerna and the creation of the ego-Self axis is that there is a physical dimension to our own experience of incarnation. If Christ is to be born within us, he must be born in our bodies as well as in our souls.

Francis's experience at LaVerna began with a vision, according to Celano's account of the miracle. We might call this vision a product of active imagination. Francis had spent so much time imaginatively interacting with the life of Christ that he experienced this interaction as a powerful vision. "He saw *in the vision of God* a man standing above him, like a seraph with six wings, his hands extended and his feet joined together and fixed to a cross. Two of the wings were extended above his head, two were extended as if for flight, and two were wrapped around the whole body."[160] Francis never analyzed the meaning of this vision. Instead he experienced its meaning through the stigmata he received. His understanding came through, and was expressed by, his body. However, Celano and many after him tried to explain its significance. Their efforts are somewhat like the recounting of a vivid dream or the description of a beautiful dance. The immediacy of the dream or the dance is dissipated in the retelling, yet its importance is honored in the telling, especially for those who experience life more intellectually than viscerally. So we will try to understand why a seraphic vision was the vehicle for Francis's transformation and by exploring some of the details of the vision, we may better understand how the psyche uses symbols to communicate its truths.

The seraph that Francis saw in his vision evokes the seraphim in Isaiah 6. In 742 BC Isaiah had a vision of God "seated on a high and lofty throne."[161] In his vision, "Seraphim were stationed above; each of them had six wings: with two they veiled their faces, with two they veiled their feet, and with two they hovered aloft."[162] However, the seraph Celano reports is different from Isaiah's vision in three important ways. First, the seraph is actually "a man like a seraph," that is, a man partaking of the heavenly attributes of an angel, just as Francis is a man about to partake of the wounds of Christ. Second, Francis's seraph is not covering its face. In fact it looks at Francis, who "rejoiced very greatly because of the kind and gracious look with which he saw himself regarded by the seraph."[163] Third, the seraph comes down to Francis and is "fixed to a cross."[164] Celano notes "the sharpness of its suffering."[165] In contrast, Isaiah's seraphim are exultant and powerful. "'Holy, holy, holy is the Lord of hosts!' they cried one to the other. 'All the earth is filled with his glory.'"[166] Isaiah's seraphim proclaim the glory of God. Francis's seraph announces God's participation in human suffering.

One of the seraphim in Isaiah's vision purifies Isaiah's mouth with an ember taken from the sacred altar of God. The seraph is preparing Isaiah for his prophetic mission. He tells the prophet, "Now that this has touched your lips, your wickedness is removed, your sin is purged."[167] Isaiah is ready to answer when God calls.

Francis's seraph also purges him of any sin. Instead of an ember from God's altar, it uses the wounds of Christ. After purgation through the stigmata, Francis's body itself becomes a prophetic statement that humans can become like Christ through total identification with his suffering.

According to Jungian understanding, "Mystical experience is experience of archetypes."[168] Francis's vision is a symbolic representation of the archetypal energy of the Self that, as a Christian, he perceives as Christ. It is the symbol of Christ, seen in the seraph, that propels his psycho-spiritual journey.

The wounding that results from the vision is also symbolic in the Jungian sense. It is a physical expression of psychic energy. Francis accessed his spirituality through the humanity of Christ; Christ's wounds express and validate this experience. They physically depict a psychic reality, what Edinger called the ego-Self axis. Francis's stigmata symbolize the connection he has made, through suffering, with the archetypal energy of Christ. Because Francis accessed his spirituality through the humanity of Christ, Christ's wounds best express and validate this experience. They physically depict the psychic reality of the connection he has made, through suffering, with the archetypal energy of Christ.

Celano interprets Francis's vision as a set of directions for effecting the same mystical experience in others. He explains each physical detail of the seraph as a specific instruction about behavior that can enable a person to achieve the same relationship to Christ as Francis did:

> We can without a doubt attain this reward, if after the manner of the seraphim, we extend two wings above our head, that is, if we have, after the example of the blessed Francis, a pure intention in all our works and if our actions are upright....These two wings must be joined together to cover the head, because the Father of lights will by no means accept the uprightness of a work without purity of intention or vice versa....The feathers of these wings are love of the Father, who saves us in his mercy, and fear of the Lord, who judges us terribly.[169]

Celano goes on to explain the other wings and feathers in terms of explicit behavior directives and analogies. The seraph becomes a visual manual instructing people how to achieve Francis's sanctification. For Francis, the seraph has the numinosity of a symbol. For Celano, it is a sign that points the way to enlightenment.

Jung believes that any product of the psyche can be perceived as either a sign or a symbol and that both interpretations are necessary as part of the individuation process. Celano interprets the seraph as a sign directing one on the road to enlightenment. This interpretation allows useful strategies for developing "the inner or outer necessities of the life process" that create "a transformation of energy."[170] Francis's numinous experience of the seraph, however, was as a symbol of the transformation of energy itself. It was the product of his direct experience of the archetypal energy of the Incarnation. As direct experience, it was beyond explication.

Jung treats the cross as a symbol rather than a sign. As symbol, the cross is an inexplicable expression of "an as yet unknown and incomprehensible fact of a mystical or transcendent, i.e., psychological, nature, which simply finds itself most appropriately represented in the cross."[171] When the cross is reduced to a simple equation with divine love or compassionate suffering or any other formula, it is being used as a sign. In contrast, as a symbol, the cross points to a mystery.

Whitmont discusses the symbolic expression of the Self in terms that further help explain Francis's mystical vision through a psychological paradigm: "This archetype [Self] expresses itself in the form of predestined wholeness of an individual life, which seeks fulfillment."[172] Since Francis sought fulfillment through compassionate identification with the humanity of the suffering Christ, the Self expressed itself in that form.

Since a symbol is unknowable by the conscious mind, its

meaning cannot be articulated. It can, however, be experienced; and it is, necessarily, experienced through the body. The body is the first frame of reference for the development of consciousness, and it "provides the basic frame of reference for symbolic experience."[173] Francis's vision was a powerful example of this truth. His symbolic experience was so fully experienced by his body that the seraph's stigmata were imprinted on his flesh. Celano explains how this occurred based on information from "a certain person,"[174] probably Brother Leo, in whom Francis confided. Francis could not understand what the vision meant and was moved by contradictory emotions. In Celano's account,

> When the blessed servant of the most High saw these things, he was filled with the greatest wonder, but he could not understand what this vision should mean. Still, he was filled with happiness and he rejoiced very greatly because of the kind and gracious look with which he saw himself regarded by the seraph, whose beauty was beyond estimation; but the fact that the seraph was fixed to a cross and the sharpness of his suffering filled Francis with fear. And so he arose, if I may so speak, sorrowful and joyful, and joy and grief were in him alternately.[175]

Francis was torn by conflicting emotions and strove for a sense of meaning that would explain this combination of beatific benevolence and physical suffering. The understanding Francis sought was not intellectual; it was spiritual and emotional: "His soul was in great anxiety" and "the vision perplexed his heart."[176] He was looking at the intersection of two levels of reality: the spirituality of a seraph and the physicality of a crucifixion. There was no way for him to understand this vision rationally. He had to experience it. At this point in Celano's account, the physical marks of the stigmata that Elias described in his letter began to appear on Francis's body, "just as he had seen them a little before in the crucified man above him."[177]

The stigmata, in which the meaning of Francis's symbolic vision is imprinted on his body rather than understood in his mind, are a miracle that can be understood in terms of synchronicity. Combs and Holland discuss the psychological basis of synchronicity: "[It is] rooted in the deepest level of the mind or psyche, the *unus mundus*. Jung referred to this level as a pseudopsychic or *psychoid* state, since it is not strictly psychic but partly physical as well."[178]

The *unus mundus* is the archetypal level of the psyche that manifests as physical symbols. The energy that is released through archetypal activation is also responsible for synchronistic events that connect the physical and psychic realms and provide a profound sense of meaningfulness through the overlap of two seemingly disconnected levels of reality. Combs and Holland's discussion of the interaction of psychic and physical phenomenon is useful at this point:

> In Jung's thinking, the activation or awakening of an archetype releases a great deal of power, analogous to splitting the atom. This power, in the immediate vicinity of the psychoid process from which the archetype takes its origin, is the catalyst for the synchronistic event. The idea is that the activation of an archetype releases patterning forces that can restructure events both in the psyche and in the external world. The restructuring occurs in an acausal fashion, operating outside the laws of causality.
>
> The power that is released is felt as numinosity—literally a sense of the divine or cosmic. It is described by Jung's student Ira Progoff as "a sense of transcendent validity, authenticity, and essential divinity."[179]

When the archetype of the Self is activated as in Francis's vision of the seraph, the energy is powerful enough to "restructure events both in the psyche and in the external world." Francis is transformed in body and soul.

The seraph in the vision gives Francis's experience a timeless quality. It connects him to the prophetic tradition of the past; it occurs in the present; and it establishes, through the stigmata, his prophetic message that God is immanent in all people, not just in Christ. Another dimension of its timelessness is its symbolic nature as an archetypal manifestation. Jacobi explains the creation of symbols in terms of archetypal energy: "The archetype as such is concentrated psychic energy....The symbol provides the mode of manifestation by which the archetype becomes discernible."[180] Archetypes exist in the unconscious; we cannot know them directly. We know them through symbols. Francis's seraph connected him to the archetypal Self.

Francis's culture believed that God was transcendent. He had become immanent in the incarnation, but that was a one-time event. In Francis's time, God could only be accessed through the sacramental life of the church. But Francis's vision at LaVerna suggested otherwise. Francis's stigmata introduced the new possibility that incarnation was possible for anyone who was able to participate in Christ's human suffering. This is Elias's "new miracle" and "joyful news" that is as relevant to us as it was to Francis.

Ewert Cousins sees Francis's vision as marking a paradigm shift in Christian mysticism. Heaven comes down to man rather than the mystic rising up to heaven. Cousins also interprets Francis's response to the seraph as marking a transformation of consciousness in which "compassion for the suffering Savior was given an archetypal expression in Francis and through him was channeled into Western devotion, art, and culture as a whole."[181] Francis became a new symbol to constellate archetypal energy.

The church was slow to promulgate the miracle of the stigmata. The miracle was not even included as evidence of Francis's sanctity during the canonization process, which occurred soon after his death. Francis's speedy canonization served to defuse the potential threat of a mere man becoming like Christ. By quickly canonizing Francis—the process was completed within two years of his death, more by acclamation than by formal inquiry—the church elevated him beyond ordinary human status. Because medieval saints "were considered superhuman with achievements that the ordinary Christian could not hope to emulate,"[182] the radical implications of Francis's total imitation of Christ were muted by his canonization. *Saint* Francis received the stigmata as a special sign of God's favor to him. The church's implicit message was that such a miracle was unique to Francis.

However, the impact of Francis's mystical experience and stigmatization for human potential was understood by Celano, who explained Francis's stigmata as something new in the relationship between people and God. This is a "new miracle" he said, "to console the minds of the weak." It uses "things visible" to create a love of "things invisible." It moves human identification with God to a new level by creating the same marks "in him who dwelt upon earth" as those displayed "in him who *descended from heaven*."[183] Celano does not limit the implications of this new miracle to the canonized Francis. Instead, he uses the seraphic vision as a pattern for replicating the experience and states with confidence that "we can without a doubt attain this reward."[184]

Celano's first interpretation of God's "new revelations" was too radical for the collective values of his day. In his revised biography of Francis, commissioned by the Franciscan minister general in 1244, Celano treats Francis as an exemplary and exalted saint from the moment of his birth, rather than as a flawed human being who evolved into an understanding and experience of his special relationship with God. Francis's superhuman perfection makes his experience at LaVerna seem inaccessible to others. Celano, earlier so clear in his interpretation of the seraph as a visual representation of the road to enlightenment, sounds tentative about the implications of Francis's experience for others by the time he reaches the end of his second account, written two decades later. He says, "Let this alone be made known to human ears that it is not yet fully clear why the mystery appeared in the saint; for, as far as it has been revealed by him, it must get its explanation and reason in the future."[185] Celano can no longer confidently articulate the implications of Francis's experience for his life or the lives of other people. The consciousness of his age cannot encompass the miraculous thing that happened to Francis, who had evolved spiritually beyond his times.[186]

Perhaps we are finally ready to understand the implications of Francis's experience at LaVerna by using Jung's theory of individuation, which is a restatement, in the language of psychology, of the mystic's journey into identification with the divine. The mystic speaks of God; Jung speaks of the Self. Yet both are describing the same reality. Jung describes the Self as "not only the centre, but also the whole circumference which embraces both conscious and unconscious; it is the centre of this totality, just as the ego is the centre of consciousness."[187] This image of the center that is also the circumference parallels the mysticism of Bonaventure, the great medieval philosopher and minister general of the Franciscan Order. God is both the essence of each soul and the transcendent goal of the soul's spiritual journey.

Bonaventure is critical to our understanding of LaVerna because he both understood the enormity of Francis's experience and tried to harness its power within the container of the church. Bonaventure was eleven years old when Francis was canonized. Unlike Celano, who was born within a few years of Francis and so grew up in a pre-Franciscan world, Bonaventure was always aware of Francis as a person of extraordinary sanctity.[188] Whereas Celano was personally in touch with the original simplicity of Franciscanism and well acquainted with several of Francis's closest followers, Bonaventure grew to understand Franciscanism through the intellectual tradition that developed at the University of Paris. Although he appreciated the simplicity that characterized Francis and his followers, he also believed that Franciscanism, like early Christianity, had to evolve to include an intellectual understanding of its implications and an institutional framework for its realization. Like St. Paul, St. Bonaventure, who as stated before is called the Second Founder of the Franciscan Order, had to translate a unique personality into a viable institution.

In 1259 Bonaventure went to LaVerna to meditate on the meaning of the miracle that had happened there over thirty years before. He had already succeeded the more radical John of Parma as minister general of the Franciscan Order and was trying to redirect the order along a more moderate path by skirting the potential heresy of its more extreme members, who wanted to insist on radical poverty as the defining Christian virtue and who questioned the necessity of the church as a channel of grace. While meditating at LaVerna, Bonaventure wrote *The Soul's Journey into God*. Cousins explains Bonaventure's use of *soul* as meaning 'the God within'—"the image of God in the depths of a person, the most profound dimension of man's spiritual being."[189] Bonaventure argues that the soul is attracted to God transcendent by the God within. For Bonaventure meditating on Francis's seraphic vision, Christ crucified is the only symbol that constellates the God within. Christ becomes the symbol of the Self that constellates the archetypal energy of the psycho-spiritual journey.

Saint Francis Receives the Stigmata by Pietro Lorenzetti
(Lower Church, S. Francesco, Assisi, Italy).

There is a tension in Bonaventure between his mystical understanding of the archetypal power of Francis's experience at LaVerna and his roles as Catholic philosopher and Franciscan administrator. Although Bonaventure believed that Francis's experience provided an experiential model for mystical illumination, he also had the task of systematizing Franciscan spirituality and incorporating it within the container of the church. Bonaventure's decision to strengthen Franciscanism as an order within the church diminished the impact of Francis as an example of individuation for Christians.

Some of the more radical thirteenth-century Franciscans believed that Francis ushered in the age of the Spirit prophesied in the twelfth century by Joachim di Fiore. Joachim believed that history had moved through the age of the transcendent Father and the age of the incarnate Son. Joachim foresaw the age of the immanent Spirit, when people would discover God within and no longer need the institutional church. Some believed that Francis's combination of contemplative mysticism and active spirituality in the secular world ushered in that new age.

A painting by Ambrogio Lorenzetti (now located in the cathedral museum in Siena) presents an interpretation of Francis's experience at LaVerna in keeping with Joachim's belief in God's immanence in the age of the Spirit. Lorenzetti, painting in 1348, almost a century after Bonaventure wrote about LaVerna, shows the seraph emerging from Francis's chest. Both Francis and the seraph are gazing in the same direction. In psychological language, the seraph is a symbol from within Francis that constellates the Self on which both now gaze. The seraph does not come down from heaven but emerges from within Francis. Centuries later, the psychological implications of Francis's experience find similar expression in Jung's theory of individuation, which insists on God's immanence as the power that fuels psycho-spiritual development.

The first extant depiction of the stigmatization, part of the Pescia dossal by Bonaventura Berlinghieri, includes the viewer in the vision at LaVerna. The dossal, a painted wooden panel, was used in the thirteenth century to depict saints. On the Pescia dossal, the central figure of Francis stresses his unique martyrdom by means of the stigmata. The scene at LaVerna is one of six events from Francis's life depicted on each side of the central figure. The seraph is identified as Christ by wounds to its hands and feet. It is connected to Francis by a golden band, but it is looking at us. The viewer is drawn into the scene by the seraph's gaze and feels, like Celano, that "we can without a doubt attain this reward"[190] by emulating Francis's identification with Christ.

Although the early iconography for depicting Francis's vision varies somewhat as artists experiment with visually effective methods, the representation stresses the availability of the beatific vision to all. After Bonaventure, frescoes replace the more intimate, interactive form of the dossal, and the communication between Francis and the seraph, rather than the viewer's inclusion in the seraph's gaze, is emphasized.[191]

After Bonaventure, the seraph also becomes more explicitly painted as Christ crucified. In pre-Bonaventure versions, the identification with Christ is only suggested by the position of the seraph's arms and feet. After Bonaventure, Christ is painted in more detail as the specific symbol needed to elicit the miracle of experiencing divinity.

As the seraph becomes more identified with Christ and diverts its gaze from the viewer, Leo comes to stand for humanity in the scene. He is usually depicted in front of a church and separated from Francis by a chasm. Leo is usually reading the Bible while Francis is having his vision. The

Saint Francis by Bonaventura Berlinghieri (S. Francesco, Pescia, Italy).

message seems to be that the church and the Bible are the path for ordinary people. Francis's experience is unique to him. For example, Giotto's depiction of Francis's stigmatization in the upper church of the Assisi Basilica, based on an inscription from Bonaventure's biography of the saint, exemplifies the iconography that evolved based on Bonaventure's biography. Francis is at his mountain hermitage, separated from Brother Leo by a chasm. Leo, sitting in front of a church, is reading the Bible. He is unaware of the vision, an occurrence outside the official scope of the church and Bible that define his physical and spiritual space. Francis is on one knee with his arms partly raised. He is in the process of receiving the stigmata. Golden rays move from the five wounds of Christ, wrapped in the wings of a seraph, to Francis's hands, feet, and side. In Giotto's fresco, Francis's seraph appears as a man with outstretched arms. The bottom half of the man, except for his feet, is covered by the seraph's middle wings. The man is looking at Francis as rays from his wounds create the stigmata. Both Francis and the man have halos. The two halos and the golden rays, as well as Francis's position and the wings of the seraph, create the impression of a holy place set apart from the rest of humanity.

In another fresco, Gregory IX, who presided over the canonization, has a dream that authenticates the stigmatization. Gregory, levitating off his bed, receives from Francis a vial of blood from his side wound. Francis exposes the side wound to the viewer. Neither Gregory nor the four other men in the painting looks at Francis. Although Gregory had this dream before Francis was canonized, he waited until after Francis had been officially declared a saint to issue papal bulls attesting to the authenticity of the stigmata. One cannot know the reason for the delay, but its effect was to minimize the danger of the laity thinking they could directly encounter God outside the sacramental life of the church.

Not all of the art mirrors official church thinking. Pietro Lorenzetti, who decorated the lower church of the Assisi Basilica about thirty years after Giotto completed the fresco cycle in the upper church and a few years before his brother painted the seraph emerging from Francis, also depicted the scene at LaVerna. His interpretation introduces new details that, like his brother's painting of Francis a few years later, suggest the archetypal, and therefore potentially universal, nature of Francis's experience. Lorenzetti dramatizes the interaction of Francis and the seraph more vividly than Giotto. The seraph, whose crucifixion is explicitly depicted by the cross and the position of arms and feet, is inclined toward Francis instead of being vertical. Its wings mirror the color of Francis's tunic instead of being the otherworldly pink of Giotto's seraph. The wings are positioned for flight, whereas the wings of Giotto's seraph are stationary. Lorenzetti's seraph suggests Christ's eagerness to join Francis in his humanity.

Lorenzetti also reinterprets both the chasm that separates Francis from Leo and the figure of Leo. A small plank connects the two sides of the chasm; and Leo, though engrossed in his book and unaware of what is happening to Francis, has a wing. Lorenzetti appears to be suggesting the potential connection of Leo (humanity) with the figures of the seraph and Francis. They form a visual triangle, and the plank and wing suggest that Leo can connect with both Francis and the seraph, the human and the divine. Leo, representing Everyman, can share in Francis's participation in divinity.

Lorenzetti's account of Francis's vision emphasizes Francis's life as a continuation of the incarnation. Read horizontally, it is the last of a series of frescoes depicting the Passion cycle. It comes immediately after a fresco of Judas hanged. Francis appears to overcome the betrayal of Judas, which is the inability of the world to receive Christ. Read vertically, Lorenzetti's seraphic Christ follows Christ at the Last Supper and Christ betrayed. For Lorenzetti, Francis's vision carries along the plan of salvation. Through Leo, humanity is part of that plan. Just as the Word was made flesh in Francis, it can be made flesh in us. Thus Lorenzetti's conception of the meaning of Francis's experience closely mirrors Jung's belief that the process of individuation calls each person to realize his or her own divine nature. Whereas the upper church fresco suggests that the incarnation only happened to Christ, and through Christ to Francis, the lower church fresco suggests the more psychologically compelling possibility that Francis's experience is a new symbol that can constellate the archetypal energy of the Self that empowers each person on the psycho-spiritual process of individuation.

Francis's experience at LaVerna, understood psychologically, changed the Incarnation from a divine event to a human possibility. As Francis experienced God's immanence in his own flesh, he gained a deeper understanding of God's immanence expressed throughout creation and offered a powerful example of individuation.

CHAPTER EIGHT
Canticle of Brother Sun

The year after he experienced the incarnation through his own body, Francis wrote the *Canticle of Brother Sun,* a hymn that uses creation to praise God. Francis had a sacramental view of nature. He believed that God was spiritually visible in a worm and in the weather, as well as in the official sacrament of the Eucharist. For Francis, everything in creation mirrored an aspect of God. Poverty, simplicity, and humility were the spiritual cloths Francis used to keep his unique mirror a clean and undistorted reflection. In his Canticle, he urged all of creation to reflect God.

Before he began his individuation journey, Francis took aesthetic delight in the surface beauty of nature. He was the subject, and nature was the object. Francis's depression was marked by an inability to appreciate the beauty of the Umbrian countryside; the objective world had lost its affective power. In the course of his journey, Francis came to see creation in a different light. He came to appreciate it in all its aspects—beautiful, benign, helpful, and frightening—because he had come to see God's immanence everywhere, even, after LaVerna, in himself.

The *Canticle* was written in 1225, the year before Francis died. Debilitated by the stigmata, weakened by his extreme asceticism and by an eye ailment that he probably received during the crusade to Damietta, Francis was in terrible health. While he was staying at San Damiano near Clare, his eyes were so weak that they could not even endure the light from a fire. Moreover, his cell was infested with mice, making sleep almost impossible. It was in the midst of this physical misery that Francis composed his hymn in praise of creation.

Francis's hymn is written in the Umbrian dialect. According to Franciscan scholar J. R. H. Moorman, it is the oldest extant poem in any modern language.[192] Although Francis was neither a scholar nor a theologian, he was a poet. He experienced God directly throughout creation. *That the Canticle of Brother Sun* was written in the language of the Umbrian people reflects the simplicity, humility, and generosity of Francis's spirituality. That it was set to music reflects his role as God's troubadour.

Although Francis, as a feeling type, did not take an intellectual approach to his understanding of God, his experience of God was often mediated through the Bible. As a man of the thirteenth century, he relied on the Bible to provide him with guidance, both when he opened it at random and when he used biblical verses to guide his rules for the order. As Celano notes, Francis's Canticle resembles the *Canticle of Praise* from the Book of Daniel in the Old Testament: "For as of old the three youths in the fiery furnace invited all the elements to praise and glorify the Creator of the universe, so also this man, filled with the spirit of God, never ceased to praise, glorify, and bless the Creator and Ruler of all things in all the elements and creatures."[193] When Azariah, Hananiah, and Mishael were thrown into the furnace by King Neduchadnezzer for refusing to worship a golden statue, they sang a song of praise in the midst of the flames.

Like Francis, Azariah accepts his God regardless of what suffering that acceptance may bring: "If our God, whom we serve, can save us from the white-hot furnace and from your hands, O King may he save us! But even if he will not, know, O king, that we will not serve your god or worship the golden statue that you set up."[194] Azariah does not know if his God "can" or "will" save them. Whether or not his God is omnipotent or kindly disposed to his well-being, Azariah knows that he, not the god of Nebuchadnezzer, is his God, and that he must honor that truth. Azariah's faithfulness is rewarded. An angel who "looks like a son of God"[195] joins them; and unharmed by the flames, they bless God and urge all of creation to join them in their praise.

Francis's Christ trusted his God with the same faith as Azariah, but he was not physically rescued from death. He was allowed to suffer and die. The last words that Christ uttered were words of despair and betrayal: "My God, my God, why have you forsaken me?"[196] No angel came to rescue Christ on the cross. So while Francis's hymn to God echoes the hymn in Daniel, it also reflects the paradoxical suffering of God incarnate.

Francis's hymn of praise, like Daniel's, begins by acknowledging the supremacy of God over his creation. Despite his numinous experience at LaVerna, Francis has avoided the psycho-spiritual danger of inflation in which the ego identifies itself with the Self and perceives itself as God. So Francis begins his hymn by addressing God with exquisite courtesy and humility:

> Most High, all-powerful, good Lord,
> Yours are the praises, the glory, the honor, and all blessing.
> To You alone, Most High, do they belong,
> and no man is worthy to mention your name.[197]

In the Book of Daniel, the young men's praises of God continue for five verses, placing God in heaven on a throne in a specifically different dimension from the rest of creation. For Francis, it is not necessary to make God exist on such a different plane; it is enough to acknowledge his supremacy. For in Francis's spirituality, as in the psychological understanding of Jung, a transcendent God is inaccessible and essentially irrelevant to one's spiritual journey. Francis has come to know God intimately through the suffering humanity of his Son. Francis's God is immanent in creation.

Francis perceives the sun as the closest mirror of God in nature. Light is one of the most powerful symbols of Christ, who is "the light of the human race"[198] and, according to Jung's psychological understanding, a symbol of human consciousness. Francis makes this close relationship of the sun to God explicit:

> Praised be you, my Lord, with all your creatures,
> especially Sir Brother Sun,
> Who is the day and through whom You give us light.
> And he is beautiful and radiant with great splendor:
> and bears a likeness of You, Most High One.[199]

Francis refers to the sun with the chivalric title *Sir* and singles him out "especially." The sun is the "day" and God's vehicle for bringing light into the world. Francis tells God that the sun "bears a great likeness to you," reminding God that he is a God of light who is "beautiful and radiant with great splendor." God is praised with the sun, the symbol of his Son who brought light into the world.

Daniel's hymn of praise does not compare God with his creation. Daniel's God is completely transcendent. He is "exalted above all forever." The hymn of praise in Daniel does not present nature sacramentally. The different aspects of creation do not have symbolic resonance. However, the sun is included in a litany of God's creation, beginning with angels and ending with the three men in the furnace. All are called upon to praise God. None have the capacity to mirror God.

Francis's experience of God's immanence in creation makes his hymn of praise different from Daniel's in another way. God's immanence creates kinship among all aspects of creation. God is the Father of the whole physical world, which makes all of creation brothers and sisters. This intimate kinship between creation and the speaker of the hymn is expressed by addressing each manifestation of creation as brother or sister. In Daniel, each aspect of creation is discrete from the three men singing in   the furnace. In his hymn, Francis is joined to all creation as brothers and sisters with the same Father. Francis speaks of Sister Moon, Brother Wind, Sister Water, Brother Fire, and Sister Mother Earth, expressions of the divine immanence.

Between the sun, which mirrors the divine light of consciousness, and the earth, which sustains and defines life's physical expression, are the moon and stars, wind and weather, water, and fire. Sister Moon and the stars are "clear and precious and beautiful." Formed in heaven, they mirror an unambiguous state of perfection not found on earth. The moon and stars are the feminine experienced from an idealized distance. In psychological language, they reflect the unconscious unity that exists before the process of individuation, a process that occurs on earth. Sister Water on earth is also precious, but her other attributes link her to earthly rather than celestial concerns. She is "very useful and humble and precious and chaste." On earth, the feminine manifests as water, which, paradoxically, though precious, is useful and humble. The feminine on earth is also chaste. It is differentiated from the masculine.

In Francis's hymn creation is presented as opposites. He praises the opposites through the air and weather as well as the polarities of masculine and feminine:

> Praised be You, my Lord, through Brother Wind,
> and through the air, cloudy and serene, and every kind of weather
> through which you give sustenance to your creatures.[200]

It is the opposites of "cloudy and serene" and the variety of
"every kind of weather" that sustains God's creatures. Francis finds God in every expression of life. He does not limit
God to that which benefits egocentric needs. In fact, he
claims that it is the extremes that *sustain* God's creatures.
The verse to Brother Wind reflects Francis's experience of
individuation through suffering. He understands and
praises a God who expresses himself through "every kind of
weather."

Brother Fire is the earthly counterpart of Brother Sun.
As Sister Water expresses the feminine as it is embodied on
earth, Brother Fire embodies the masculine. Like Brother
Sun, he is beautiful; but his other attributes are less remote
than the sun's radiance and splendor:

> Praised be You, my Lord, through Brother Fire,
> through whom you light the night
> and he is beautiful and playful and robust and strong.[201]

Brother Fire is there when the sun seems gone. He is for
the dark times, which he dispels through play rather than
through splendor. He is "robust and strong." He does not
mirror God as "Most High One," but rather God as he is
experienced during night on earth. Brother Fire, like the
sun, is beautiful; however, his beauty is set off by discrimi-
nating his light from the darkness. The sun manifests in the
day. Brother Fire is the light that manifests in the darkness.

Francis's original *Canticle* ends with Sister Mother Earth
who, like the sun, plays a special role in mediating the relationship between God and creation. Earth has a double title
(like the sun whose double title "Sir Brother" is a paradox that

suggests both a higher rank in creation and a sense of kinship). Earth is Sister but also Mother to creation. As Mother
she has a triple role. She sustains, governs, and produces:

> Praised be You, my Lord, through our Sister Mother Earth,
> who sustains and governs us,
> and who produces varied fruits
> with colored flowers and herbs.[202]

Mother Earth maintains life but also controls its expression
by providing parameters. Francis affirms the goodness of
life on earth by capturing its essence in the image of "var-
ied fruits with colored flowers and herbs." Within the
earth's governance, there is variety: fruit, which both sustains life and is pleasant to eat; flowers, which bring beauty;
and herbs, which flavor life.

The goodness of variety in creation is a fundamental
premise of Franciscanism. God's immanence is most fully
expressed in the uniqueness of each of its many manifestations. What is true for vegetation is also true for human
life. In psychological language, it is only through the
uniqueness of a life realized through the process of individuation that the Self can express itself through the ego.
Francis's mystical vision of God's immanence in every
aspect of creation mirrors his experience of inner divinity
through the process of individuation.

Mother Earth in Francis's hymn provides all that is
needed for the maintenance of life, but she has her laws that
govern her sustenance. Perception of these laws (with obvi-
ous ecological implications) includes parameters for psycho-
spiritual development. Francis urged his followers to
discover their own spirituality, but he warned against what
Celano calls "singularity" and Jung calls "individualism."
Celano gives an account of a brother who was deemed a
saint by the other friars because of his constant prayer and

total silence, including his refusal to confess his sins except by sign language. Francis intuited that this supposed saint was thoroughly dedicated to cultivating his peculiarities rather than to developing his spirituality. When ordered to break his silence to participate in the sacrament of confession, the friar refused. He subsequently "left religion of his own accord, went back to the world, returned *to his vomit.*"203

Jung similarly warned against cultivating idiosyncrasies at the expense of collective needs. Like Francis, he perceived that the Self can only manifest through the particular, but he shared Francis's insight that idiosyncrasies should be recognized but not exalted. According to Jung, "Individualism means deliberately stressing and giving prominence to some supposed peculiarity rather than to collective considerations and obligations. But individuation means precisely the better and more complete fulfillment of the collective qualities of the human being."204 The paradox is that God is praised through uniqueness when that uniqueness is dedicated to praising God.

In Francis's hymn, God is praised for and through and by his creation. There is a deeper level of intimacy among Francis, God, and creation than existed for the three young men in Daniel. The complexity of the relationship between God and his world is suggested in Umbrian by the word *per,* which is a preposition with several possible translations. According to Armstrong and Brady, "It may be translated 'for,' suggesting an attitude of thanksgiving; 'by,' expressing a sense of instrumentality; or 'through,' indicating instrumentality as well as a deeper sense of mysticism in perceiving God's presence in all creation."205 Francis's hymn suggests all three meanings of praise. There is gratitude for the attributes of creation, the capacity of creation to glorify God through these attributes, and an experience of God's immanence through creation.

Boff interprets the *Canticle of Brother Sun* as "the expression of a reconciled universe that was taking place within the heart of Francis."[206] Through the power of introverted sensation, Francis experienced the outer world through the subjective filter of his inner serenity. However, soon after the *Canticle* was completed, Assisi was once again torn apart by civil strife that once again thrust Francis into the world of action as a man of peace. Bishop Guido excommunicated the head of the commune, the *podesta* (chief magistrate), who in turn issued an economic blockade against the bishop. Francis added a verse to his *Canticle* and had it sung to the podesta and other civil officials in the bishop's palace:

> Praised be You, my Lord, through those who give pardon for
> Your love
> and bear infirmity and tribulation.
> Blessed are those who endure in peace
> for by You, Most High, they shall be crowned.[207]

The bishop and the podesta embraced, forgetting, for the moment at least, their differences.

Dourley comments on the power of inner work to transform the world: "Mystics who have achieved some high degree of the union of opposites within themselves may then become vehicles of resolution of social and political conflict beyond them."[208] Francis's acceptance of suffering as the medium of transformation became an example for the people of Assisi. For a brief time at least, they were willing to overcome their egocentric needs and effect a peace that transcended their differences.

The final section of the *Canticle* was written as Francis was dying:

> Praised be You, my Lord, through our Sister Bodily Death,
> from whom no living man can escape.
> Woe to those who die in mortal sin.

Blessed are those whom death will find in Your most holy will,
for the second death shall do them no harm.
Praise and bless my Lord and give Him thanks and serve Him
with great humility.[209]

Francis accepts even death as his sister. Earlier in his journey he experienced the feminine as Lady Poverty and as the Virgin, as well as the physicality of Christ's incarnation and suffering. In the outer world, he experienced the feminine through Clare and Lady Jacoba, as well as through the moon and stars, water, and Mother Earth. Now, as he was about to die, he experienced the feminine as the force that ends life. Mother Earth "sustains and governs," and part of her governing is to decree that bodily life is finite. Death is another manifestation of God that Francis accepts as inevitable. He has no expectation of deliverance. Instead he perceives Sister Death as another way to both experience and praise God.

Like the second section of the *Canticle,* the final section on death demonstrates Francis's consciousness that he must set an example for others. He needs to share what he has learned on his journey, so he articulates the two attitudes to death and their repercussions. For those who die "in mortal sin"—that is, irrevocably estranged from God through lack of consciousness of divine immanence—there is "woe." For those whom death finds "doing Your will"—that is, expressing God's immanence through, in psychological language, the process of individuation—there is blessedness.

The blessedness of those who are doing God's will when they die derives from their invincibility to "the second death." Sister Bodily Death, the first death, is a finite part of the created world. The second death, described in John's apocalyptic vision, eternally consumes whatever eludes consciousness of God's absolute immanence. Those who have done God's will experience the new age prophesied by John in the first century (as well as by Joachim di Fiore in the twelfth, and Carl Jung in the twentieth): "Behold, God's dwelling is with the human race. He will dwell with them and they will be his people and God himself will always be with them [as their God]. He will wipe every tear from their eyes, and there shall be no more death or mourning, wailing or pain [for] the old order has passed away."[210]

Francis's spiritual journey brought him to the new order. Freed from the final egocentric fear, the fear of physical death, his own ego was so connected to the unconscious through the symbol of Christ that he had arrived at his destination, where "the former heaven and the former earth had passed away, and the sea was no more."[211] The sea, symbol of the unconscious, was no more, because everything had been brought to consciousness. Through suffering, Francis had arrived at the level of consciousness where "God's dwelling is with the human race"; and through his example, he hoped to encourage others to suffer, in their own way, a journey into the unitive consciousness in which God and all creation are one.

CHAPTER NINE
The Hero's Journey

This book began with the image of Francis as a garden
statue. We have taken him out of the garden and examined
the journey that enabled him to constellate powerful energy
for many people during his lifetime and beyond. Through
the centuries, much of Francis's energy has become unavail-
able to us as Western consciousness has moved through the
Reformation, the Enlightenment, the Scientific and Indus-
trial Revolutions, and a twentieth century of unprecedented
materialism, bloodshed, and violence. And yet, at the end
of this century, there is renewed interest in St. Francis. In
1980 Pope Paul II named Francis Patron of Ecology. In 1982
Francis's eight-hundredth birthday was celebrated. In 1986
the world's religious leaders chose Francis's Porziuncula as
the best place for an ecumenical gathering. Books, articles,
web sites, and Franciscan communities all attest to the growing influence of St. Francis. Why does Francis speak so
compellingly to us as a new millennium begins?

I suspect that the contemporary appeal of such a
medieval curiosity as St. Francis of Assisi lies partly in the
nature of his quest. Francis set out, like his boyhood hero
St. George, to slay dragons in the world.[212] He discovered
that the only monsters worth his struggle lay within his own
soul and that the fair damsel in need of rescue was within
himself as well. We who are fearfully peering into the

twenty-first century are in particular need of a hero who dares to undertake both the outer and the inner journey.

In *The Hero with a Thousand Faces,* Joseph Campbell discusses the quest of the modern hero as the conquest of himself. Although the hero's quest has always been to subdue the Other—be that natural or supernatural forces, wild animals, or human enemies—Campbell contends that "the center of gravity, that is to say, of the realm of mystery and danger has definitely shifted....Man is that alien presence with whom the forces of egoism must come to terms, through whom the ego is to be crucified and resurrected, and in whose image society is to be reformed."[213] The struggle must be carried on within each unique human life. *Who are you, God? and who am I?* is the nature of the modern hero's quest. Francis is a hero for our times.

Francis's journey has the satisfying literalness of travel from one place to another. It did not just happen in his head and heart. With Francis we go back to the physical origins of the metaphor of spiritual journey. We have that aha! experience that refreshes a hackneyed phrase. Francis's journey carried him throughout Italy and to Spain and the East. It started and ended outside Assisi. It was both a physical journey through the world of spirit and a spiritual journey through the world of creation. It included the three phases of the archetypal quest—departure, initiation, and return—on both a physical and a spiritual level. Francis as a hero speaks to the urgent need to both change the world by changing ourselves and change ourselves by changing the world.[214]

A hero like Francis transforms the collective understanding of heroism. Had Francis accepted his culture's definition of heroism, he would have continued on his journey from Spoleto and fought against the infidel as an armed knight. He would have departed from Assisi on a literal level but would have carried his city's values into battle. His initiation would have been trials of physical and mental endurance, and his return, assuming victory in battle, would have been as a knight who had vanquished a physical foe. However, Francis's heroic journey had the psychological implications of the mythic tales explored by Joseph Campbell. It was a journey of spiritual transformation and growth, happening in space and time.

The situation that precipitated the physical departure of Francis on his quest, his repudiation of his father, was the outer expression of the dis-ease that precipitates the growth of consciousness. In the earliest state of consciousness, we are unaware of the division between the conscious and the unconscious; and we accept our conscious standpoint, fashioned by our family and culture, as the ultimate truth. We believe that our persona is an adequate expression of our personality. Like Francis, we must depart from this comfortable belief.

Francis's hero quest is illuminated by Christian mythology. When Adam and Eve ate from the Tree of Knowledge, they became conscious of the polarities in creation, including Creator/creation, obedience/disobedience, dependence/autonomy, good/evil, life/death, and male/female. They departed from the primal unity. We all experience this departure on a physical level through birth and separation from our mother. Physically and emotionally united throughout pregnancy and infancy, mother and child symbolize the principle of eros, visually depicted in Western culture through the Madonna and Child. One or both gaze at the viewer, inviting us to regain their serene unity.

In Christian mythology, the child first returns to his mother as the broken figure of Jesus in the *Pietra,* like the dying Francis in the arms of Lady Jacoba, seemingly the victim of the heroic quest. But because Christ and Francis accept Sister Death as an inevitable part of the journey, both are transfigured as they enter into the kingdom of

God, the unitive vision that overcomes physical death. Both are recognized as sons of God, Christ through his resurrection and Francis through his stigmata. Their acceptance of death transforms others as well. According to the Catholic doctrine that made Jung so jubilant about healing the Godhead, Mary is taken into heaven to rejoin her son, prefiguring our own resurrection. And Lady Jacoba, representing each of us, "drew new life from her deceased friend" and urged that the stigmata, symbols of our own potential unity with Christ, be "unveiled before the eyes of all."[215]

In mythic terms, the father represents *thanatos,* the death that destroys primal unity. In the Christian myth, God the father turns on Adam, forcing him to leave Eden. He visits Job with unwarranted suffering. And he allows the death of his only son. Francis's father also forces Francis to leave the naive simplicity of his early life and to be separated from his mother. This destructive role of the father is crucial to the hero's quest. Only through the death of the old can the new be born. The destructive power of the father is as critical to psycho-spiritual growth as is the vision of unity provided by the mother. Francis rejected his physical father and placed total reliance on God. His literal departure from Assisi took two years. His psycho-spiritual departure occurred with the renunciation of his father.

Campbell calls the first stage in the hero's departure "the call to adventure." An adventure takes us far from the person we are familiar with to new dimensions of our being. A modern myth of the call to adventure occurs in *The Hobbit* when the self-satisfied Bilbo Baggins must leave the comforts of his well-furnished hobbit hole and heed the call to become—of all things—a burglar. In Francis's case, the sensual, well-dressed darling of Assisi must become an ascetic vagabond dressed in rags, preaching poverty as the way to salvation. Francis's poverty and Bilbo's burglary on behalf of dwarves are both tangible expressions of the spiritual need to be unencumbered on the hero's quest. Both Francis and Bilbo are in love with their possessions. They must lose this attachment if they are to be reborn.

The notion of impoverishment as a prerequisite for heroism is a bit odd. We, like the young Francis, imagine heroism embellished with the accoutrements of power and protection. But if the true act of heroism is to look in the mirror and see what is there, we must strip away all our defensive trappings. Then, just as in hero myths throughout the world, we will receive supernatural or synchronistic assistance. A talking cross, Lady Poverty, biblical passages, and a variety of animals all helped Francis understand his journey. The point of the hero's receiving supernatural help underscores the inadequacy of our conscious standpoint to equip us for the journey. Alone we cannot successfully depart from the familiar and embark on a journey into the unknown. We need, and will receive, help from the psycho-spiritual realm.

The transformation of the conscious personality occurs in the depths of the unconscious. Jonah is swallowed by a whale. Joseph is put in a well. Francis hides in the pit at San Damiano. What is important to us about the structure of the call to adventure is to realize that our ego will urge us to refuse all the signs that beckon us forward. We will want to refuse change, for it is frightening. But we have no choice. The puzzle of our life is missing many crucial pieces, pieces that can only be recovered by an inner journey.[216] And we are not alone. The Virgin, Hermes the Trickster, Francis's Lady Poverty, or whoever our journey requires will appear to guide us.

With supernatural support, the hero is ready to cross what Campbell calls "the first threshold." This threshold moves the hero beyond the world of the senses and the inevitability of death. It is guarded by a fearsome creature. For Francis, the horror at the threshold was a leper. Before he crossed the threshold, he was trapped in a world of opposites: poverty and wealth, beauty and ugliness, sickness and health, life and death. When he crossed the threshold by kissing the leper, he left his sense-bound ego behind.

Once the hero has made his departure, he undergoes an initiation into the paradoxical nature of reality, the second phase of the journey. He learns that his conscious ego has its unconscious counterpart which, if he opposes it, contradicts his conscious image and goals. His life up to this point has been fashioned around his conscious understanding. Now he must suffer the rest of the puzzle by allowing material from the unconscious to fall into place as well. In religious language, this is the daily crucifixion of the ego that we all must undergo in the process of individuation.

The other side of the threshold is the new, strange world in which the hero undergoes his initiation into the union of opposites and a unitive vision of reality. The hero embarks on what Campbell calls "the road of trials." The psycho-spiritual purpose of these trials is to sublimate the ego to a higher purpose. Campbell stresses the multiplicity of the hero's trials and describes the ego as a many-headed Hydra—"one head cut off, two more appear."[217] In the Christian myth, Job embodies this phase of the hero quest. The hero must conquer any sense of pride in his own accomplishments and accept the power of the irrational Other.[218] He must recognize that his sorrow, like his accomplishments, are caused by something beyond his conscious will. Only a total renunciation of control can pave the way for the hero's return.

Francis experienced the other side of the threshold as a place of constant battle with his ego. He castigated himself as a miserable sinner and a worm.[219] He inflicted public penances on himself. Still the hydra sprouted new heads. All the while, as Campbell describes it, "there will be a multitude of preliminary victories, unretainable ecstasies, and momentary glimpses of the wonderful land."[220] Celano documents these moments in Francis's life as visions, healings, and clairvoyant understanding. However, it is not these glimpses that bring the hero to his destination. It is rather the utter poverty and humility of spirit that brings the hero to an acceptance of his utter worthlessness. Francis called this "perfect joy" and described it in a conversation with Brother Leo.

He began by describing all that is *not* perfect joy. Paradoxically, his list included all the goals one could reasonably desire for the friars: holiness, miracles, prophecy, knowledge, conversion of infidels, and a list of further accomplishments that, according to the account in *The Little Flowers of St. Francis,* continued for two more miles of their walk. Instead, perfect joy is willing acceptance of tribulations as unwarranted as those of Job. Francis described perfect joy as being rejected and castigated upon their return home because "above all the graces and gifts of the Holy Spirit which Christ gives to his friends is that of conquering oneself and willingly enduring sufferings, insults, humiliations and hardships for the love of Christ."[221] The "road of trials" leads the hero to an understanding of this paradoxical perfect joy, the complete purgation of egocentricity.

It is important that we understand that the hero's journey consists of endless mini-journeys. Each time we think that the ego is a vehicle for the Self or that Christ lives fully within us, the hydra sprouts another head and we must depart once more. In Franciscan spirituality, this constant battle is called *metanoia,* a daily conversion of the human will from self-interest to God.

The hero's return is the sharing of the spoils with the people he left behind when he began his quest. It is the broadening and deepening of our collective consciousness that justifies the hero's departure from collective norms.

The traditional knight would bring home booty from plundered cities. Francis brought back a direct experience of Christ's incarnation working through himself and all creation. He showed that incarnation is a human possibility, but he could not make it happen for other people. Campbell observes, "The boon brought from the transcendent deep becomes quickly rationalized into nonentity, and the need becomes great for another hero to refresh the world."[222] We institutionalize our heroes and turn them into statues. Instead, we need to use their energy and insights to empower us as we heroically live into our unique incarnation in our own space and time.

What is most important to *us* in the heroic journey of a thirteenth-century saint? Perhaps it is the need for introversion to balance the extraversion of our age. The thirteenth century was an age of pervasive collective values. The church provided a structure of beliefs and assumptions similar in power to the effects of television and the internet and mass culture. Everyone was plugged into the same defining experiences. The church was the mass media of the thirteenth century. To question the assumptions of extraverted values required then, as it does today, an inner journey. Francis was a hero as well as a saint. He took his unique relationship to his inner truth out into the world. He accepted the reality of his world, but he believed it could be transformed by an infusion of interior values.

The proliferation of garden statuary of Francis suggests that we in the twentieth century find Francis a compelling image. Whether we can create and sustain his post-Edenic garden, relying as it does on the courage of consciousness, depends on our willingness to heroically suffer, like Francis, the process of individuation.

Conclusion

Francis of Assisi was called to discover how a thirteenth-century person could pattern his life on the archetypal energy of Christ. At the beginning of his journey, Francis was told, "Rebuild my Church." His journey led him from a literal interpretation of that task, when he rebuilt the walls of crumbling churches around Assisi, to a symbolic understanding when his own life became a new channel for archetypal energy. As Ewert Cousins observes, "For Western culture as a whole Francis has become the symbol of the religious sense of the divine immanence."[223]

Francis's experience of "the divine immanence" deepened his empathy for all of creation. By discovering the divinity within himself and expressing it as fully as he could, he became conscious of the divinity in every other aspect of creation. In the process, he had to withdraw his projections from other people and things. He had to accept every dimension of himself in order to see the world as it really is rather than as he wanted or expected it to be. Beginning with his kiss of the leper and ending with the embrace of Lady Jacoba, Francis's journey to the spirit was through the flesh that he so feared and despised. His journey is witness to Jung's discovery, centuries later, that God is most present in that which we hate and fear.

Francis's psycho-spiritual journey enabled him to infuse

old forms and symbols with new life, the life that came from his direct experience of the numinous. Both the uniqueness and the influence of Francis's life testify to the distance he traveled on his inner journey. In *Psychology of Transference,* Jung, quoting from a sixteenth-century alchemical text, describes the attributes of one who is able to undergo the transformation of individuation: "He who would be initiated into this art and secret wisdom must put away the vice of arrogance, must be devout, deep-witted, humane toward his fellows, of a cheerful countenance and a happy disposition, and respectful withal. Likewise he must be an observer of the eternal secrets that are revealed to him."[224] The humble, reverent, courteous, joyful man from Assisi, carrying the marks of "the eternal secrets" revealed to him at LaVerna, was initiated into the "art and secret wisdom" and became a hero of the journey out of the garden.

Notes

INTRODUCTION

1. Carl G. Jung, "The Development of Personality," in *The Choice Is Always Ours*, ed. Dorothy Berkley Philips, Elizabeth Boyden Howes, and Lucille M. Nixon (San Francisco: Harper, 1975), 64–65.

2. Caroline Walker Bynum, *Holy Feast and Holy Fast: The Religious Significance of Food to Medieval Women* (Berkeley: University of California Press, 1986), 299.

3. John P. Dourley, *Love, Celibacy, and the Inner Marriage* (Toronto: Inner City Books, 1987), 25.

4. Matthew 10:9, *The New American Bible*, Saint Joseph ed. (New York: Catholic Book Publishing Co., 1991). All biblical texts will be quoted from this version.

5. The *animus* is the masculine dimension of a woman's psyche. Post-Jungians are currently revising their understanding of the animus.

I. COLLECTIVE VALUES IN THE THIRTEENTH CENTURY

6. In the thirteenth century, the laity were seldom permitted to receive communion. Even monks and nuns were severely limited.

7. The rivalry between Guelphs and Ghibellines originated in territorial disputes in twelfth-century Germany. In thirteenth-century Italy, the rivalries became political, with the Guelphs supporting the pope and the Ghibellines the emperor.

8. One explanation for the phenomenon of the Crusades is

the pressure of too many noblemen's sons in Europe. With not enough land to go around and not enough priestly and monastic openings, many noblemen engaged in pillaging and warfare. The Crusades provided an opportunity to fight the heathen instead of fellow Christians and the possibility of acquiring new lands to settle in the East.

9. Monasticism had its worldly side both in its vast land holdings and in its socio-economic function as a dumping ground for extra sons of the nobility for whom there was not enough land to go around.

10. William R. Cook and Ronald B. Herzman, *The Medieval Worldview: An Introduction* (New York: Oxford University Press, 1983), 241.

11. Daryl Sharp, *C. G. Jung Lexicon: A Primer of Terms & Concepts* (Toronto: Inner City Books, 1991), 68–69 (from CW 18).

12. Renata Blumenfeld-Kosinski and Timea Szell, eds., *Images of Sainthood in Medieval Europe* (Ithaca, N.Y.: Cornell University Press, 1991), 4.

II. ADAPTATION AS THE MERCHANT'S SON

13. Sharp, 14 (from CW 6).

14. Ibid., 99 (from CW 7).

15. Arnaldo Fortini, *Francis of Assisi*, (New York: Crossroad, 1981), 158.

16. Thomas of Celano, *St. Francis of Assisi* (Chicago: Franciscan Herald Press, 1963), I:1.

17. Ibid., I:2.

18. Ibid., I:17.

19. Nikos Kazantzakis. *Saint Francis* (New York: Simon & Schuster, 1962), 31.

III. STRIPPING OFF THE PERSONA

20. Sharp, 98 (from CW 7).

21. Edward C. Whitmont believes that depression is "based on

the ego's notion that it should be in control of life" (*The Symbolic Quest: Basic Concepts in Analytical Psychology* [Princeton: Princeton University Press, 1969], 249).

22. Celano I:3.

23. Bonaventure, *The Soul's Journey into God. The Tree of Life. The Life of Saint Francis* (New York: Paulist, 1978), 187.

24. Sharp, 121 (from CW 4).

25. Ibid., 120 (from CW 7).

26. Celano I:3. Francis would later move from an aesthetic to a spiritual appreciation of the natural world.

27. Art historians argue about whether the frescoes in the upper church of the Assisi Basilica were painted by Giotto or by members of his school.

28. Frati Minori Conventuali. "Vita di S. Francesco Legli affreschi della Basilica Superiore in Assisi," (Assisi: Casa Editrice Francescan, 1987), no. 2.

29. Whitmont, 156.

30. Frati Minori Conventuali, no. 3.

31. Fortini, 188–189.

32. Celano I:6.

33. Sharp, 119.

34. Celano I:6.

35. Ibid.

36. Ibid., I:8.

37. Ibid., I:9.

38. Ibid., I:11.

39. Ibid.

40. Ibid., I:13.

41. Ibid.

42. Sharp, 50.

43. Ibid. (from CW 6).

44. Celano, I:13.

45. Edward F. Edinger, *Ego and Archetype* (New York: G. P. Putnam & Sons, 1972), 49.

46. Sharp, 112 (from CW 9i).

47. Bishop Guido had to try Francis's case when his father accused him of disobedience—he was still legally a minor—and of

squandering his family's resources. Assisi's consul could not try Francis because, having sought the church's protection at San Damiano, he was no longer subject to secular authority.

48. Frati Conventuali Minori, no. 5.
49. Whitmont, 220.
50. Celano I:15.

IV. LOOKING AT THE SHADOW

51. Sharp, 123.
52. The ritual of the mass has some of this same power. The community channels its sense of sinfulness and estrangement through the priest, who reenacts Christ's sacrifice and heals the rift between sinners and their God.
53. Fortini uses a thirteenth-century document as the basis of his imaginative description of the church's ritualistic separation of lepers from the rest of society and asserts that the chivalric code did not extend to lepers. Francis was well within his culture's bounds in being horrified by lepers.
54. Celano I:17.
55. Celano II:9.
56. Joseph Campbell, ed., *The Portable Jung* (New York: Penguin Books, 1971), 145–6.
57. Ibid., 145.
58. Marion A. Habig, ed., *St. Francis of Assisi: Writing and Early Biographies: English Omnibus of the Sources for the Life of St. Francis*, trans. Rachel Brown et al., 4th rev. ed. (Quincy, Ill.: Franciscan Press, 1991), 67.
59. Celano II:9.
60. Campbell, *The Portable Jung*, 146.
61. Celano II:129.
62. Ibid.
63. Ibid., 112.
64. Ibid.
65. Ibid., 114.
66. Ibid., 205.
67. Ibid., 207.

68. Ibid.

69. Ingrid J. Peterson, O.S.F., *Clare of Assisi: A Biographical Study* (Quincy, Ill.: Franciscan Press, 1993), 94.

70. Ibid., 94–95.

71. Ibid., 94.

72. Ibid.

73. John Sanford, ed., *Fritz Kunkel: Selected Writings* (New York: Paulist, 1984), 8.

74. Filippo Graziani, ed., *The Little Flowers of the Glorious St. Francis and of His Friars* (Assisi: Edizioni Porziuncula, 1982), 77.

75. Ibid.

76. Ibid., 78.

77. Sharp, 37.

78. Graziani, 78.

79. Ibid.

80. Ibid.

81. Ibid.

82. Ibid.

83. Ibid., 79–80.

84. Ibid., 80.

85. Although the legend of the wolf sounds apocryphal, it may have some basis in fact; the skeleton of a wolf was recently discovered during excavations in Gubbio. Francis's encounter with the sultan is widely accepted as historical fact. Hans Eberhard Mayer includes an account of it in his historical analysis of the Crusades (*The Crusades* [Oxford: Oxford University Press, 1990], 224).

86. Frati Minori Conventuali, no. 11.

V. FEMININE ENERGY

87. Whitmont, 191.

88. Celano I:13.

89. Whitmont, 193.

90. Ibid., 191.

91. Ibid.

92. Celano I:19–20.

93. Ibid., *Treatise:*37.

94. Ibid., 38.

95. Sharp, 21.

96. Celano *Treatise*:39.

97. Ibid.

98. Ibid., II:6.

99. Ibid.

100. Ibid., II:9.

101. Ibid.

102. Sharp, 94 (from CW 7).

103. Celano II:57.

104. Medieval iconography used the almond shape of the *mandorla,* the space created by the overlapping of two circles as in a Venn diagram, to enclose the Virgin and Christ. Placing the Virgin in a mandorla symbolizes her role as the intersection of spirit and matter. I am indebted to Robert Johnson for introducing me to the image and concept of mandorla.

105. Regis J. Armstrong, O.F.M. Cap., and Ignatius C. Brady, O.F.M., ed. and trans., *Francis and Clare: The Complete Works* (New York: Paulist, 1982), 149. Pope John Paul II's attempt to make a dogmatic assertion about the Virgin's coequal role with Christ in the process of redemption can be interpreted as a manifestation of the psychic need to incorporate the feminine into the Godhead.

106. Jung sometimes discussed the cross as an image that incorporates the shadow side of God in the person of Jesus' evil brother. The quaternity of the cross represents Father, two Sons, and Holy Spirit.

107. Sharp, 110 (from CW 16).

108. Celano II: 203.

109. Peterson, 186.

110. Frati Minori Conventuali, no. 13.

111. Ewert Cousins, "Francis of Assisi and Christian Mysticism," in *Mysticism and Religious Traditions*, ed. Steven T. Katz (Oxford: Oxford University Press, 1983), 168.

112. Sharp, 13 (from CW 14).

113. Ibid.

114. Ibid.

115. Ibid.

116. Cousins, 166.

117. Celano I:80.

118. Armstrong and Brady, 152.

119. C. G. Jung, *Psychology and Religion: West and East,* trans. R. F. C. Hull, Bollinger Series XX, (New York: Pantheon Books, 1958), 179–80.

120. Armstrong and Brady, 152.

121. Ibid.

122. Jung is ambivalent about the nature of what he calls "the missing fourth" in the Godhead. While he rejoices in the Virgin's assumption into heaven, his model of quaternity based on the cross seems to more consistently favor the dark rather than the feminine side of God. Jung is also unable to conceive of the feminine as part of the Trinity because, based on natural imagery, the Trinity should be Father, Mother, and Son, not Father, Son, Mother/Holy Spirit. Jung cannot accept the feminine as the third person because the Holy Spirit emanates from Father and Son, masculine energy. However, in Greek mythology, Wisdom, in the person of Athena, was generated from Zeus, so there seems to be archetypal support for feminine Wisdom emerging from masculine energy. These examples, coupled with his inadequate description of a woman's animus, suggest some limitations in Jung's understanding of the power of the feminine in human consciousness as well as in a woman's personal unconscious.

123. Armstrong and Brady, 61.

124. Habig, 72.

125. Armstrong and Brady, 46. Bernard of Clairvaux initiated the feminization of religious language and authority in the twelfth century for cloistered monks, but Francis moved Bernard's insights about the feminine aspects of spirituality and relationship into the secular world by modeling maternal love among his mendicant friars.

126. Habig, 977.

127. Sharp, 22–23 (from CW 7).

128. Ibid., 77 (from CW 10).

129. Francis was following his intuitive feeling about the situation when he tried to convert the sultan. Matthew 10, which was

the biblical source of his evangelical mission, enjoins the apostles, "Do not go into pagan territory or enter a Samaritan town. Go rather to the lost sheep of the house of Israel" (vv. 5, 6). At his best, Francis interpreted the Bible and the teachings of the church according to his own authentic assessment of the situation in front of him. When he tried to slavishly follow rules and regulations according to some rigid mental logic, his moral authority and effectiveness were diminished (see chapter 6).

VI. REMOVING THE BLINDERS

130. Jung was an introvert. His autobiography, *Memories, Dreams, Reflections,* has very little about the external events in his life, concerning itself instead with his inner journey.

131. Women could be more introverted than men because more of their life could occur in the relatively private world of the home. Clare's immediate family consisted of a group of deeply spiritual women. Her father having died, she lived with her mother and some aunts.

132. Celano I:91.

133. Habig, 67.

134. The base of the San Damiano cross is interesting to consider in the light of individuation. Several figures are below Christ's feet with only the upper part of their bodies showing. The shell pattern that encloses the rest of the figures is absent from the bottom of the cross. It is as if the figures at the base of the cross are partway on their journey into Christ's kingdom. I am indebted to Rev. Sartor, O.F.M. Conv., for bringing the bottom of the cross to my attention.

135. Campbell, *The Portable Jung*, 182.

136. Thirteenth-century iconography provides visual documentation of the shift in consciousness. Contrast the serene figure of Christ on the cross from San Damiano with the iconographical convention of Francis at the foot of the cross embracing the bleeding feet of the suffering Christ. This shift results from what was described earlier as historical mysticism. A subjective consciousness interacts with an historical event, and in

the process, it develops new psycho-spiritual understanding and relationship with the Self. This process is an example of the transcendent function that arises from the tension between conscious and unconscious material and gives birth to a new level of consciousness.

137. According to Peterson, Clare's mother undertook a pilgrimage to Jerusalem.

138. *Synchronicity* is another interpretation of the world that is based in part on introverted sensation. Events in the outer world correspond to psychic reality as they are filtered through the subjective consciousness of an individual attuned to acausal relationships. Modern physics support the notion of a close relationship between mind and matter, contending that the observer affects the outcome of any subatomic event that is being monitored.

139. Habig, 67.

140. Campbell, *The Portable Jung*, 224.

141. Fortini, 98–100. According to Fortini, on St. Nicholas Day there was a special kind of play acting. All social conventions in Assisi were turned upside down. On that feast day, a boy impersonated the bishop and even performed a mock mass in the cathedral. This custom, which lasted until the seventeenth century, was observed to licentious excess in Francis's time, supporting Celano's contention that Francis grew up in a corrupt social environment. It is interesting to wonder if Francis ever acted the part of the bishop.

142. Campbell, *The Portable Jung*, 224.

143. Matthew 12: 46–50, NAB.

144. Campbell, *The Portable Jung*, 225.

145. Celano I:40. Extreme mortification was not unusual in the Middle Ages.

146. Ibid., II:65.

147. Jung refers to the stigmata as a means of transforming saints into Christ figures who "symbolize the workings of the Holy Ghost among men" (Jung, *Psychology and Religion*, 185).

148. Campbell, *The Portable Jung*, 224.

149. It is interesting that we have only the sketchiest record of Francis's sermons. People were moved by the experience of hear-

ing him speak, but they rarely felt compelled to record what he actually said. He appealed to their hearts rather than their heads. Some of his surviving writings sound didactic and dogmatic when he is using his thinking rather than his feeling function. When he writes from the heart, as in the beginning of his *Testament* and his canticles, we get a better idea of why his sermons were so effective.

150. Bonaventure, sometimes called the Second Founder of the Franciscan Order, took over in 1257. He had a different psychological orientation from Francis. Although he was profoundly inspired by Francis's unique relationship with Christ, he had the logic of a thinking type and the practicality of a sensing type when it came to implementing Franciscan spirituality. In this he was like St. Paul, who translated Jesus' vision into an institutional church. Much was lost in both translations, but without Bonaventure and Paul, the visions of Francis and Jesus might not have survived in any form at all.

VII. LAVERNA

151. Brother Elias was an intellectual educated at the University of Bologna. It was he who had the grand basilica built in Assisi to honor Francis, the saint of poverty and humility. He was eventually ostracized from the order for his ostentatious lifestyle and excommunicated for political intrigue.

152. Edward Edinger adopts E. Neumann's term *ego-self axis* as a metaphor for the critical flow of energy needed if the ego is to remain healthy and develop a higher level of consciousness. The religious term for the ego-self axis is *grace*. Edward Edinger, *Ego and Archetype* (New York: G. P. Putnam & Sons, 1972).

153. William R. Cook, *Francis of Assisi*, Vol. 8, *The Way of the Christian Mystics* (Wilmington, Del.: Michael Glazier, Inc., 1989), 94.

154. *The New American Desk Encyclopedia* (New York: Penguin, 1989), 827.

155. Campbell, *The Portable Jung*, 505.

156. Sharp, 133 (from CW 8).

157. Synchronicity is akin to introverted sensation. The subjective consciousness filters the physical sensation through a

framework of meaning.

158. Jung, 185.

159. The objective reality of a talking cross is not the issue. What matters here is Francis's need to hear an outer voice tell him what to do before he could hear the voice within.

160. Celano I:94.

161. Isaiah 6:2, NAB.

162. Isaiah 6:4, NAB.

163. Celano I:94.

164. Ibid.

165. Ibid.

166. Isaiah 6:3, NAB.

167. Isaiah 6:2, NAB.

168. Dourley, 45.

169. Celano I:114.

170. Sharp, 131 (from CW 8).

171. Ibid.

172. Whitmont, 219.

173. Ibid., 275.

174. Celano, I:90.

175. Ibid., I:94.

176. Ibid.

177. Ibid.

178. Allan Combs and Mark Holland, *Synchronicity, Science, Myth, and the Trickster* (New York: Paragon House, 1990), 69.

179. Ibid., 74.

180. Quoted in Whitmont, 118.

181. Cousins, "Francis of Assisi and Christian Mysticism," 175.

182. Blumenfeld-Kosinsk and Szell, 2.

183. Celano I:114.

184. Ibid.

185. Ibid., II:203.

186. Francis's experience, which can be understood as constellating a new level of archetypal energy from within the Self, was too far ahead of the cultural paradigm of the thirteenth century to be accepted. Meister Eckhart, who understood and preached Francis's radical new experience of God's immanence,

was labeled a heretic. It is interesting to imagine what would have happened if the Spirituals had retained power within the Franciscan Order. Their understanding of the mystical journey anticipates Jung's by hundreds of years. Dourley notes the close identification of Jung's psycho-spiritual interpretation of life with that of Joachim di Fiore: "Jung comes very close to presenting himself and his vision as a modern reincarnation of Joachim di Fiore, the twelfth century monk who proclaimed the nearness of the age of the Spirit, when humanity and divinity would thoroughly pervade each other and God would be all in all" (p. 94). Neither the collective psyche of the thirteenth century nor its social institutions was ready for the radical implications of God's immanence implicit in Francis's psycho-spiritual journey, though some individuals understood its meaning for human potential.

187. Sharp, 119 (from CW 12).

188. Bonaventure believed that St. Francis had miraculously intervened when he was dying of a serious disease as a young boy (4–5).

189. Ibid., 21.

190. Celano I:114.

191. The Siena dossal, painted in 1280, is an exception. There may have been more visual depictions of Francis's experience that support a psycho-spiritual interpretation of LaVerna. Most medieval art has disappeared. Also, this interpretation may have been suppressed. Bonaventure had Celano's biographies of St. Francis destroyed. Only a few, located in the libraries of other religious orders, survived.

VIII. CANTICLE OF BROTHER SUN

192. Habig, 128.

193. Celano I:80.

194. Daniel 3:17–18, NAB.

195. Daniel 3:25, NAB.

196. Matthew 27:46, NAB.

197. Armstrong and Brady, 38.

198. John 1:3, NAB.

199. Armstrong and Brady, 38.

200. Ibid., 39.

201. Ibid.

202. Ibid.

203. Celano II:28.

204. Sharp, 66 (from CW 7).

205. Armstrong and Brady, 38.

206. Leonardo Boff, *Saint Francis: A Model for Human Liberation*, trans. John W. Diercksmeir (New York: Crossroad., 1984), 42.

207. Armstrong and Brady, 39.

208. Dourley, 51.

209. Armstrong and Brady, 12-14.

210. Revelation 21:3-4, NAB.

211. Revelation 21:1-2.

IX. THE HERO'S JOURNEY

212. Fortini tells us that a painting of St. George dominated the little schoolroom attached to San Giorgio where Francis was educated.

213. Joseph Campbell, *The Hero with a Thousand Faces*, 2nd ed., Bollingen Series XVII (Princeton: Princeton University Press, 1968), 390–91. Campbell believes that the hero's quest is always essentially the same. He quotes the Vedas: "Truth is one, the sages speak of it by many names" (p. viii). Campbell substantiates this insight by documenting the parallels among hero quests, using the language of psychoanalysis to decipher their shared symbolic natures.

214. Because Francis is the example of heroism being used, I will use the masculine term *hero* throughout my discussion. However, many women also undertake both an inner and an outer journey as they experience psycho-spiritual individuation. For women, the father often precipitates departure through his powerlessness to protect her rather than through confrontation. The impotence of the masculine in her outer world forces her on a journey to discover another source of strength. Many fairy tales

begin with this absence of masculine energy.

215. Celano, Treatise:39.

216. For the jigsaw puzzle metaphor to explain repression I am indebted to David Cox (*Jung and St. Paul: A Study of the Doctrine of Justification by Faith and Its Relation to the Concept of Individuation* [New York: Association Press, 1959]).

217. Campbell, *The Hero with a Thousand Faces*, 114.

218. Jung reads Job as a catalyst to God's consciousness. Job's perseverance under God's bullying reveals a greatness in the human spirit that God can only access by becoming human himself ("Answer to Job," in *Psychology and Religion: West and East*, 357–470).

219. When praised for his saintliness, Francis responded, "I can still have sons and daughters; do not praise me as being secure" (Celano II:133). Woman both personified his goal, through Lady Poverty, the Virgin, and St. Clare, and provided his greatest temptation along the "road of trials."

220. Campbell, *The Hero with a Thousand Faces*, 109.

221. Fortini, 485–6.

222. Campbell, *The Hero with a Thousand Faces*, 218.

CONCLUSION

223. Ewert Cousins, *Bonaventure and the Coincidence of Opposites* (Chicago: Franciscan Herald Press, 1978), 247.

224. Sharp, Frontispiece.

Glossary

Active imagination. A conscious interaction with symbols of unconscious energy. The religious term for active imagination is *prayer*. Francis developed a special form of active imagination in which a person imaginatively and emotionally participated in events in the life of Christ as a means of accessing a connection with the divine or, in psychological terms, the unconscious.

Adaptation. The process of conforming thoughts, feelings, and behavior to collective standards. What is unacceptable to collective norms is either not brought to consciousness or is repressed. Adaptation is a necessary stage in developing ego strength. It must, however, be subordinated to the process of individuation if an authentic, mature personality is to develop.

Affect. A strong emotional response triggered by a person, idea, object, or event, which symbolizes unconscious psychic energy. For example, Francis was moved by any representation of a cross.

Anima. The feminine side of a man's psyche. It is encountered through dreams and is projected onto women. It is also expressed collectively through female icons in the cultural, mythological, or religious spheres. Jung sometimes used *anima* as a synonym for *soul*. Anima is associated with the eros principle of relatedness.

Archetypes. Universal patterns of unconscious psychic energy that come to the attention of consciousness through dreams, prayers, active imagination, creativity, projections, symbols, and rituals. Because archetypes exist in the unconscious, they cannot, by definition, be known directly by the conscious ego. For both Jung and Francis, Christ crucified was the most powerful symbol of the opposites that constitute the paradoxical nature of archetypal unity.

Collective unconscious. Refers to patterns of psychic energy common to all people at all times. It includes archetypal energy experienced as God, mother, father, lover, and other broad categories of human experience and relationship.

Compensation. The tendency of the psyche to balance conscious and unconscious experiences. Psychic energy consists of opposites. Any conscious thought, feeling, or action is immediately compensated in the unconscious by its opposite. For instance, a generous action constellates an unconscious impulse to niggardliness or a tyrannical attitude in public is compensated by a weak unconscious posture. Robert Johnson uses the image of the teeter-totter to describe compensation. A person must straddle both sides to keep his or her balance. Because the unconscious does not discriminate between real and symbolic acts, this balance can be kept through ritualistic or creative acts rather than by literal enactment of the destructive impulses of the psyche.

Complex. Refers to an emotionally charged response to an idea, person, object, or event. When a complex is activated, the person reacts unconsciously, with strong affect, regardless of how s/he might consciously choose to respond.

Constellate. To activate a complex.

Consciousness. An activity that grows out of unconsciousness from the experience of opposites. Consciousness is regulated by the ego. It is that part of the psyche that the ego knows and allows to exist.

Crucifixion. A symbol that constellates psychic energy involving opposites and their resolution.

Depression. The absence of conscious energy that occurs when psychic energy is deflected to the unconscious. The purpose of depression is to bring to consciousness unconscious material needed to compensate the conscious attitude.

Dreams. Autonomous products of the unconscious. Using symbols, they describe the unconscious attitude and/or the potential of the unconscious to compensate for the conscious attitude.

Ego. The center of consciousness. It is also the conduit for unconsciousness. It must be strong enough to withstand the power of archetypal energy and flexible enough to accommodate growth. It requires masculine energy to maintain its integrity and feminine energy to grow. During individuation, the ego must suffer a conscious relationship to the persona, anima, and shadow and must experience itself as subordinate to the Self.

Egocentricity. Fritz Kunkel's term for the ego's unwillingness to acknowledge the reality of anything that is not already part of consciousness. Egocentricity is the chief impediment to individuation.

Extraversion. The movement of psychic energy toward the outer world of people and objects.

Feeling. The psychological process that determines the worth of what is perceived.

Functions. Sensation, intuition, thinking, and feeling are the four functions that, coupled with extraversion and introversion, provide our psychological orientation. Sensation and intuition inform us about what does or could exist. Thinking and feeling help us interpret what we perceive. A person's primary function is the one s/he is most comfortable using. The inferior function is least available to consciousness. It is always the opposite of the primary function. For example, when sensation is primary, intuition is inferior; when feeling is primary, thinking is inferior. The other two functions are auxiliary; they assist the primary function.

Individuation. The process of overcoming egocentricity by accepting and honoring the shadow, the anima (animus in a woman), and the Self without losing the ego as the center of consciousness. Individuation separates a person from collective values by dictating a unique path through life. It is teleological; the goal is the creation of an authentic personality. It is redemptive; salvation occurs through incarnation of the Self in the ego and the ego's life in the world.

Inflation. An exaggerated sense of one's importance, resulting from a numinous experience of the unconscious, uncompensated by a real or symbolic act of humility. Francis had the psychological insight to realize that he needed to go work with lepers after his vision at LaVerna.

Introversion. The movement of psychic energy toward the inner world.

Intuition. The psychological process that perceives the possibilities inherent in a situation.

Numinous. Applies to dreams, projections, symbols, or rituals that constellate the unitive psychic energy of the Self and elicit powerful affect.

Persona. Both a person's conception of herself and the picture she presents to the world. *Persona* comes from the Greek word for 'mask.' Persona is a product of adaptation. One of the tasks of individuation is to make the ego conscious of, rather than identified with, the persona.

Personal unconscious. Refers to patterns of psychic energy unique to a given individual. It is that part of the unconscious psyche that is determined by nature and nurture rather than by the fact of being human.

Personality. The expression of the ego differentiated from the collective values of the persona. One of the goals of individuation is the development of authentic personality. Jung sometimes used *personality* as a synonym for *soul.*

Projection. The unconscious process of seeing oneself in someone or something else. The ego must become conscious of what is projected if it is to become aware of the totality of the personality. Francis projected his own share of divinity onto Christ until he received the stigmata.

Psyche. The term for all conscious and unconscious psychological processes.

Quaternity. An image of wholeness containing four parts. The cross is an example of quarternity. The four men in the fiery furnace in the book of Daniel is another. Jung believed that Christianity was incomplete because it conceived of God as Trinity rather than quaternity. He thought that the doctrine of the assumption of the Virgin into heaven moved Christianity in the direction of wholeness.

Repress. To move from consciousness to unconsciousness in the interests of adaptation or to protect the ego from what is too powerful for it to contain. It is a form of denial.

Self. The archetypal energy of wholeness that Jung called "the God within." The ego develops from the Self, which transcends limitations of space and time. The Self is symbolized by quaternity. It is both the center and the circumference of the psyche.

Sensation. The psychological process that perceives on the basis of the physical senses.

Shadow. Refers to aspects of oneself that have either been repressed during adaptation or have never been actualized. The shadow compensates for the persona. It is experienced as the Other. The shadow is encountered in personal dreams and projections, as well as collectively as the enemy or devil.

Symbol. Refers to a person, object, or event that gives form to archetypal energy. The symbol is not synonymous with the archetype. Rather, it is its incarnation.

Synchronicity. A meaningful acausal relationship between psychic and physical events. The phenomenon of the stigmata, which is first documented with Francis, is an example of synchronicity. Synchronicity suggests a continuum between the spiritual and physical levels of reality.

Thinking. The psychological function that interprets perceptions.

Typology. Jung's classification of personality according to the movement of psychic energy (inner or outer), coupled with the availability to consciousness of sensory perceptions, intuitive perceptions, cognition, and valuing.